A CENTURY OF

KINDERGARTEN EDUCATION

IN ONTARIO,

1887 to 1987

by

Barbara E. Corbett

THE FROEBEL FOUNDATION
1576 Dundas Street West
Mississauga, Ontario
L5C 1E5

Frontispiece; "Chapter 38, An Act to Amend the Act respecting
the Education Department, 1887," obtained from the Provincial Archives
of Ontario and reproduced with the kind permission of the Queen's Printer for Ontario.

First Printing - January 1989

I S B N   0 9690587 3 X

Published by
The Froebel Foundation
1576 Dundas Street, West
Mississauga, Ontario
Canada
L5C 1E5

Printed in Canada

DEDICATION

*To all educators
who share in the development
of the whole child.*

FOREWORD

As an educator, Friedrich Froebel was a century and a half before his time. In his kindergarten he created a model for early childhood education that was child-centred with an experiential learning program that was matched to the developmental needs of each child. In his *Education of Man* he projected a similar approach to all levels of education, including university. However, it was not until the Hall-Denis Report *Living and Learning* in 1968 that the focus of schooling for older students began to be re-oriented from rote content mastery to process learning. To approach education from a process perspective in which curriculum content is used as a means of helping the individual create an ever expanding sense of self in relationship to the rest of the world, is a Froebelian legacy.

Above all else, Froebel valued the integrity and worth of the individual child for each was a child of God. God was the creative symbol of the inherent unity and inter-connectedness among all living things and the natural environment. Contained within that unity lay the recognition of the uniqueness of every aspect of creation. Froebel saw education as a means of helping each child create a sense of self that valued and developed individual qualities while allowing each to experience through play and activity the interdependence that leads to awareness, responsibility and action. As a part of God's creation the child became a part of all humanity linked to both the past and the future.

The Froebelian kindergarten was grafted onto an existing 19th century public school system that was based on, and essentially limited to, the classics. The influence of the Kindergarten Movement permeated the system resulting in greater child-centred, activity-based learning that encouraged the inclusion in the curriculum of programs in music, drama, technical training, experimental sciences, and more recently, in the move to experiential learning in co-op credit programs that combine academic study and practical experience. However, over the years, much of Froebel's understanding about the relationship between activity and learning has been lost. Public pressures have pushed the school system back towards the older model of education for uniformity and common testing.

This book is about more than kindergarten education. Barbara Corbett has used her experience in the Froebel Kindergarten and School in Mississauga to place in contemporary terms Froebel's basic concepts of unity, diversity and continuity as

iv

educational goals that apply at all levels. In doing so, she has provided the philosophic framework for involving students actively in the learning process. Through play the young child expresses meaning and internalizes the concepts of family, work and social roles; through an approach to learning that provides active engagement in daily life the older child and adult can express, extend and modify those impressions gained in childhood.

This book should make a difference in the way people understand the learning process and work with children, whether as classroom teachers, mentors, advisors or counsellors. The contribution this book makes is to return the focus of education to the process of helping the learner find ways of expressing his/her inner nature in the external world and of internalizing the outer world so that the individual can truly become self-active, creative and responsible.

W. James Baker, B.A., A.T., Ed.D.

AUTHOR'S PREFACE

The original work for this book was undertaken during the 1960's as part of a doctoral program at the University of Toronto. While investigating and researching the introduction and development of the kindergarten in Ontario, I was introduced to Froebel's philosophy and practices. At work in libraries or down in dusty storage rooms of Board offices I felt, when I read about Froebelian views of education that I had entered *a land of milk and honey*, Froebel's educational attitudes and practices were so sensible and wholesome. During that same period I had the unique privilege of meeting and talking with men and women who were retired or who were actively helping to shape public kindergarten education in Ontario. Educators are indebted to them all for the time and effort they have given Ontario's children. I have included in the Appendix the names of people I originally interviewed and to whom I owe an untold debt of gratitude.

There were some special people I met while studying the Froebelian kindergarten and travelling in Ontario visiting School Boards and kindergartens. One such family was the Lunde family of Chicago. Laura Hughes Lunde (1887-1966) was the daughter of James L. Hughes and Ada Marean Hughes, two people largely responsible for bringing the Froebel kindergarten to Ontario. Ada Marean Hughes was Ontario's pioneer kindergartner. Laura Lunde was generous with her time and in her correspondence, sharing with me family memories as well as papers belonging to her parents. What a privilege it was, to read through her mother's kindergarten notes taken during the 1870's while she was studying with Maria Kraus-Boelte in New York to be a Froebel kindergartner. Erling Lunde, Laura's husband, continued to support my research until his death in the 1970's. Chester Lunde, their son, his wife Grace and daughter Anne, have continued to share most graciously their time and memories with me. Thus, the Lunde family have given to me a precious gift; through them I have felt a living and vital link with the early history of kindergarten education in Ontario.

Another memory I have from the '60's is meeting Mary Macintyre. Mary Macintyre was the Director of the Model Kindergarten at the Normal School in Toronto from 1892 to 1932. She was over 90 and her memory had failed her when I met her but she was still able to recall her professional experience. Her comment was, "Yes, I love children." Claire Senior Burke was another special person who encouraged me to continue my studies by her positive example and helpfulness.

Elizabeth St. John, former librarian at the Toronto Normal School, supplied me with books and suggested resources. Her mother was also a Froebel trained kindergartner.

When I undertook this study a number of retired kindergartners who knew the Hughes family were still living. They not only shared with me their memories but they entertained me over tea and luncheons. In my experience kindergarten teachers are a giving, outgoing and gracious group. It was a privilege to meet so many wonderful people, all willing to be helpful. They were so positive in their encouragement of an emerging study of the kindergarten that I was carried in times of discouragement to endure the rigors of graduate studies by their enthusiasm.

Our Froebel Foundation in Mississauga, begun in 1970, is based on the theories and practices of Friedrich Froebel introduced to me when I was a student. Therefore, an acknowledgement of thanks to all who have contributed to this book would not be complete without an expression of appreciation to the Froebel staff who labour together so diligently and lovingly to develop our children.

May this book be a small contribution towards understanding our Froebelian educational heritage in Ontario and may it help us to be thankful for 100 years of a progressive approach to education which seeks to develop the whole child.

Barbara Elizabeth Corbett
January, 1989
Froebel House
Mississauga, Ontario

FRONTISPIECE

Ontario *Revised Statutes,* II, 1887, p.2384
An Act of the Province of Ontario establishing Kindergartens
and providing grants. Assented to 23rd April, 1887.

CHAPTER 38.

An Act to Amend the Act respecting the Education Department.

[Assented to 23rd April, 1887.

HER MAJESTY, by and with the advice and consent of the Legislative Assembly of the Province of Ontario, enacts as follows :—

1. Section 4 of *The Act respecting the Education Depart-ment,* is hereby amended, by adding thereto the following sub-sections :— <small>48 V. c. 48, s. 4, amended.</small>

(17.) To make regulations for the study of agriculture and for scientific instruction as to the nature of alcoholic stimulants and narcotics, with special reference to their effect upon the human system, and to authorize for the use of teachers and pupils, suitable text-books in said subjects, respectively, for use in all schools under the direction of the Department. <small>Instruction as to agriculture and the nature of alcoholic stimulants and narcotics.</small>

(18.) To make regulations for the organization of schools for children between three and five years of age, to be known as Kindergarten <small>Establishment of Kindergarten Schools.</small>

Kindergarten Schools ; to provide for the training and licensing of teachers for such schools, and to pay for their maintenance out of any appropriation made by the Legislative Assembly for Public Schools, such sums of money as such Kindergarten Schools may be entitled to receive on the basis of average attendance.

Ontario's Pioneer Kindergartner, Ada Marean (later Hughes)
seated centre of middle row (1883 or 1884).

Toronto students studying to be Froebelian Kindergartners.
Left to right. Back row; Carrie Lawson, ? .
Middle row; Ida Armstrong, Ada Marean, Louise Currie.
Front row; Edith Dawkins, ? , Bruce Nudel.

Courtesy of Laura Hughes Lunde.

CONTENTS

Dedication iii

Foreword iv

Author's Preface vi

Frontispiece viii

Tables xii

Introduction 1

I   Early Childhood Education, Beginnings 4
    Early Childhood Education in Britain 5
    Early Childhood Education in the United States................9

II Friedrich Froebel's Kindergarten..................................16
    Metaphysics - Froebel's Doctrine of Unity 16
    Froebel's Concept of Child Development and the Curriculum.......18
    Froebel's View of Creativity 28
    Froebel's Method 30
    Froebel's Equipment and Materials, The Gifts and Art
        Occupations 35

III Early History of the Froebelian Kindergarten in Ontario,
    1883 to 1913 39

IV The Educational Theories and Practices of The Early Kindergarten....53
    The Froebelian Doctrine of Unity 53
    Views of Child Development and the Curriculum.................54
    Creativity 63
    Educational Methods 64
    Equipment and Materials......................................67
    Summary: A Comparison of the Early Kindergarten in
        Ontario with Froebel's Kindergarten 68

V   Changing Educational Theory and Practice: The Transition Years,
    1914 to 1939 71
    The Kindergarten-Primary Movement 71
    Maria Montessori's Influence in Ontario 73
    The Influence of the Institute of Child Study,
        University of Toronto 76
    The Free Play Movement 78

VI   Continued Growth of Early Childhood Education in Ontario,
1939 to 1967 83
       Junior Kindergartens 87
       Kindergartens for the Rural School Child 88

VII   Educational Theory and Practice of the Mid-Century Kindergarten 90
       Aims in the Kindergarten 90
       Views of Child Development and the Curriculum 92
       Views of Creativity 100
       Methods in the Kindergarten 101
       Kindergarten Equipment and Materials 104

VIII   The Emerging Pattern 106
       Similarities Between the Historical and Mid-Century
         Kindergarten 106
       Differences Between the Early and Later Kindergarten 110

IX   Observations and Implications...115
       Some Observations 115
       Implications 116
       The Play Method of Kindergarten Education 117
       The Metaphysical Basis of Unity for Kindergarten Education 120

X   The Twenty Years from 1967 to 1987 125
       A Unified Educational System from Kindergarten
         Through College and University 125
       Child Development and the Curriculum 131
       The Method of Kindergarten Education: Play 135
       The Kindergartner's Role 139
       The Education of Kindergartners 143
       The Task Ahead...145

       Appendix...148
       Bibliography 151

TABLES

1.   Aims of Kindergarten Teachers and Kindergarten-
      Primary Supervisors in Ontario, 1965 to 1966. 91

2.   Similarities and Differences Between the Froebelian
      Kindergarten Introduced into Ontario and theMid-Century
      Kindergarten 114

INTRODUCTION

A child's earliest education, both in the home and in the school, has been recognized as most significant in his development, for the early years are the formative years.[1] The child not only undergoes rapid physical changes which are indicative of the rapid changes taking place in all aspects of his development, but during these early years he forms initial impressions. He outwardly may resemble the members of his family or other children his own age, but inwardly he is unique in all the possibilities of his development as well as in the ways he responds to the major occurrences and to the daily happenings in his life. These early years are crucial, for we know, and psychological research supports the claim, that the experiences of a child from birth to the age of six or seven do have far-reaching consequences.

Early childhood education in the school system includes the programs for children from ages three to seven. There are nursery schools, junior kindergartens, senior kindergartens and the primary grades of one and two. Not all public school systems in Canada provide kindergartens, although most have supported education for five-year-olds. At the present time nursery schools in Canada are private rather than part of a public school system, although more and more school boards have been providing junior kindergartens, certainly in Ontario.

The development of early childhood education in Canada is a story yet to be told. In a nation such as ours, where education is a provincial responsibility, developments within each province must first be recounted before any generalizations can be made which would apply to the country. A history of early childhood education in Canada, therefore, will be a compilation of its growth and development within each province.

Most public school systems in the United States have kindergartens for four- and five-year-old children. Research in the United States has always shown the positive influence of kindergarten experience on the child's physical development, social adjustment and later academic achievement.[2] In 1965, the American Government initiated *Operation Headstart* as a means of expanding the existing state programs for early childhood education. Its purpose was to provide three- and four-year-old children from disadvantaged homes with nursery care or junior kindergarten experiences. American educators hoped that by means of their programs, the opportunities afforded the disadvantaged child would be more nearly equal to that of a child from a middle class or better home. The television

---

[1]In order to give equal emphasis to the child as a girl or a boy the pronouns *she* and *he* are used alternately in each chapter, beginning with *he*.

[2]Neith Headley, *The Kindergarten: Its Place in the Program of Education* , New York: The Centre for Applied Research in Education, Inc., 1965, pp. 33-38.

program *Sesame Street* was introduced at that time as part of the program.

The Froebelian kindergarten made its first appearance as a private institution. It was introduced into Ontario during the 1870's, but became part of the public school system during the 1880's. Therefore, Ontario is a province with a unique history of early childhood education.

In 1887, Ontario was the first province in Canada and, for that matter, one of the first governments in the world to recognize and support kindergartens for four- and five-year-old children as part of the public school system.[3] The inclusion of the younger children came at a much later date. During the 1940's, Ottawa and Toronto extended their early childhood education programs by providing kindergartens for many of their three and four-year-old children.

Friedrich Froebel (1782-1852), the founder of the kindergarten, conceived it as the foundation of the public school system. His kindergarten was for children aged three to seven, the years now included in early childhood education. Froebel was truly an educational architect, for he planned the child's education through progressive stages of development, from the foundation years in the kindergarten to years of maturity at the university.

Froebel's followers realized the tremendous possibilities of having the kindergarten as the foundation of the structure of public education. Together with the followers of Johann Heinrich Pestalozzi (1746-1827), a Swiss educator who had been greatly influenced by the Geneva-born philosopher, Jean Jacques Rousseau (1712-1778), they helped stimulate a movement called the "New Education".[4] Its purpose was to focus attention upon the child and the importance of his development; its method, to educate the child through his own activity. In the twentieth century, the views of the New Educationists, although somewhat altered, have been upheld by the progressives in education.

Although the kindergarten from its earliest days was not easily understood nor accepted, Froebelian ideas have influenced Canadian education. Froebelian philosophy and practice, due to their early introduction into Ontario, are an important part of the development of education in this province. For example, by the turn of the century manual training, domestic science and nature study were introduced into curricula; more emphasis was placed upon the child and his development and less upon the mere learning of subject matter. Froebel's philosophical concept of unity lent support to a move toward the correlation of subject matter; educators

---

[3] In Europe, infant schools received some government support as early as the first half of the nineteenth century (*infra*, p. 4).

[4] Johann Friedrich Herbart (1776-1841), the German educator, influenced the movement as well, but not until the end of the nineteenth century in North America.

began to see the merits of a system of education which utilized the child's own activity in the learning process; and, finally, there was a new awareness that education could be a pleasant experience and school a cheerful place.[5] That there was this broader climate, the climate of the New Education, making its impression upon Canadian education, should not be forgotten in looking at the Kindergarten Movement in Ontario.

There is no doubt that the child's early years are of the utmost importance in his growth and development and that the school has a significant role to play. It was Froebel's intention that the kindergarten would include children aged three to seven and that during those years the foundation of their education would be laid. However, before discussing Froebel's kindergarten and its introduction into Ontario and thus into Canada, brief consideration will be given to the beginnings of early childhood education and its subsequent development both in Britain and in the United States because of their influence upon Canadian education.

---

[5] Charles E. Phillips, *The Development of Education in Canada,* Toronto: W. J. Gage & Co., Ltd., 1957, p. 424.

CHAPTER I

EARLY CHILDHOOD EDUCATION, BEGINNINGS

There are two significant roots to early childhood education, one sociological and the other educational. The industrial revolution brought to light a need which had always existed, the need to provide care for small children left alone because their mothers worked outside the home. Infant education in England grew out of that pressing sociological need. However, child nurture means more than physical care and protection, for it also includes the need of every child to be fully developed. It was this need that Friedrich Froebel addressed in his educational plan .

Early childhood education must also be considered within the context of two related ideas which grew out of the Reformation of the sixteenth century, for these two ideas revolutionized the educational world. The first, that all men were created equal before God, was basic to a later understanding of democracy. The second, that every man, therefore, should be able to read and interpret the scriptures for himself, implied a system of universal education. These two concepts have now been accepted in theory if not always in practice. The most recent trend in Western countries has been to refine and extend educational systems upwards as well as downwards. Thus, gradually, a setting has been created which makes early childhood education possible within a public school system.

Although educators had long been aware of the importance of the early years,[1] John Amos Comenius (1592-1670), a Moravian priest, was the first to write a special work about the training of infants. It was entitled *The School of Infancy.* In his book Comenius expressed the view that seeds of knowledge should be planted early in the child's life. He suggested that the child should learn from real things, that pictures were only second best. He would encourage a child to learn through both activity and play. Comenius believed that the young child received his or her early education at the mother's knee and did not suggest a school setting.

Jean Fredric Oberlin was the first to open a school for infants. This he did in 1769 in Waldbach, Alsace. Two French women, influenced by Oberlin's work, opened a *salle d'asile*, an infant school for refugee children, in 1826 in Paris. In 1833, such infant classes were accepted as part of the French national education system, although they later became known as *les écoles maternelles.*[2] Another early

---

[1]Plato spoke of the value of nursery training. Both Aristotle and Quintilian referred to the significance of the young child's play. See Robert R. Rusk, *A History of Infant Education*, 2nd. ed. rev.; London: University of London Press Ltd., 1951, p. 1.

[2]In 1848 *la salle d'asile* was called *l'école maternelle*, but the former name was used

infant school was one sponsored by Princess Pauline of Lippe in 1802 in Detmold, Germany.

Early Childhood Education in Britain

The first British infant school, opened by Robert Owen in 1816 in New Lanark, Scotland, became a pattern for other infant schools. James Buchanan,[3] the first master of Owen's infant school, left Scotland to establish the Westminster Free Day Infant Asylum in England. He explained Owen's ideas to Samuel Wilderspin, who did much to popularize the infant school idea in England and who, in 1824, founded the first Infant School Society. In Scotland the Glasgow Infant School Society was founded in 1827 by David Stow. Thus the British tradition of early childhood education began with the infant school. In the 1830's, largely due to the efforts of the British Home and Colonial Infant School Society, the idea came to Canada. Infant Schools were opened in Quebec, Montreal and Charlottetown.

Infant schools offered some care and training for children aged two to six who might otherwise be left to

themselves or on the streets. The children in the infant schools were supervised in their play and given some moral training. The better infant schools had a gallery which would seat as many as forty children. The master used natural objects and pictures to teach them. Singing was considered important. Some children were taught to sew, knit or garden; and the older ones were taught the three R's. Out on the playground the children were provided with gymnastic equipment on which they could play.

Private funds were donated to build and operate the first infant schools. During the 1840's, some government money was given to aid in the building of such schools. In 1862, a system of grants was introduced which had a profound effect upon the curriculum of infant schools. The new grant system became known as "payment by results". According to this system six-year-old children were required to pass the examinations of the first standard before a school could receive the grant. Therefore, school managers, to be sure of their grant, felt the three R's should be taught to the younger children even if it meant that other activities were neglected. In 1871, the examination age was raised to seven and by the 1890's the system was terminated, but by then the three R's were deeply entrenched in the infant school curriculum.

The Froebelian kindergarten was introduced into England in 1854 at the London Exhibition of the Royal Society of Arts. Those responsible for the display were Baroness von Marenholtz-Bülow, who had been a

---

again in 1855. It was in 1881 that the name *l'école maternelle* was finally adopted.

[3] In England, care for infants had been provided in the dame schools. These were run by elderly widows who needed the income. The dame schools disappeared after the Education Act of 1870.

close friend of Froebel, and Madame Ronge and Herr Hoffman, who were former students of Froebel. The Reverend M. Mitchell attended the London Exhibition and gave an account of the display, describing the Froebelian system as one well-suited to childhood. "The child is taught little; it simply produces for itself." He concluded his account by recommending that interested persons should visit Madame Ronge's kindergarten in London.[4]

Madame Ronge's kindergarten proved to be an asset to the Froebelian cause in England, for it provided a practical demonstration of the Froebelian kindergarten.[5] Charles Dickens, among others, visited her kindergarten. He then wrote an article entitled "Infant Gardens" in support of Froebel's system.[6] James L. Hughes of Toronto later referred to it as "one of the most comprehensive articles ever written on the kindergarten philosophy".[7]

While Froebelian ideas influenced British infant schools, kindergartens were introduced only through private schools. The Education Department in England expressed interest in the Froebelian system, but when young children in the infant schools were taught the three R's under the "payment by results" system, little use could be made of Froebelian theories and practices.[8] Supporters of Froebel's views, including those responsible for the founding of the National Froebel Foundation in 1887, worked very hard to make Froebelian ideas and the kindergarten more widely known so that, by the 1890's, the Education Department was giving some support to Froebelian principles.

S. J. Curtis, in his *History of Education in Great Britain*, noted that Froebelian ideas made slow progress in England and suggested several reasons for this. First of all, the idea came from a foreign source; secondly, there were no translations of Froebel's works available until the end of the century. And, thirdly, and probably the most significant reason of all, by the end of

---

[4] "Minutes of the Committee of Council on Education for 1854-5," Report by the Rev. M. Mitchell, pp. 473-74, cited by Rusk, *A History of Infant Education*, pp. 177-78.

[5] Madame Ronge was assisted in the kindergarten by Maria Boelte, who later emigrated to the United States where she opened a kindergarten and began training kindergartners (*infra*, p. 7).

[6] John Manning has expressed doubts that Dickens ever wrote the article in *Dickens on Education*, Toronto: University of Toronto Press, 1959, pp. 131- 32.

[7] James L. Hughes, *Dickens as an Educator* , New York: D. Appleton & Co., 1913, p. 3.

[8] In 1899 the Education Department became the Board of Education and in 1944 the Board of Education became the Ministry of Education. A new name was adopted in 1964 when the Ministry became the Department of Education and Science.

the nineteenth century the three R's were a part of the infant school curriculum. Curtis believed Froebelian influences had a greater impact on the English infant school at a later date through the writings of the American educator, Professor John Dewey.[9]

There were three further developments during the first part of the twentieth century which influenced infant education in Britain. The first of these was the Child Study Movement which was begun in the United States under the leadership of Professor G. Stanley Hall of Chicago University. The second was a system of education for children aged three to six which was developed by Dr. Maria Montessori in Rome, Italy. The third was the Nursery School Movement which was introduced in England by Rachel and Margaret McMillan.

Supporters of the Child Study Movement in Britain began to question the fine Froebelian handwork and the smallness of the Froebelian equipment. They considered the fine muscle activity too detailed for a young child in view of the findings in child study that large muscle development preceded fine muscle development. They also criticized Froebel's singing games and plays as being too restrictive for the child. As a result, the detailed handwork of the Froebelian art occupations was discarded and replaced by freer types of art work. Large muscle activity was introduced in place of play with the Froebelian toys. Jungle gyms, ladders, slides and tricycles, as well as sand and water play, were introduced. Gradually, all of Froebel's games and plays were replaced by a freer type of play. Mildly disputed in Britain, the questions raised by the supporters of child study precipitated a sharp division in the American Kindergarten Movement[10] (*infra*, p. 11).

During the early part of the twentieth century, many lecturers in teacher training institutes emphasized Froebelian methodology, although changes were gradually brought in. For example, Miss M. E. Findlay, a lecturer at the Froebel Educational Institute in Roehampton, studied for three years in the United States where she came under the influence of Professors Hall and Dewey. Yet on her return to the Froebel Institute, she continued to advocate that a child learns best through her own activity. Through the years Froebelian colleges have placed the major emphasis upon child development and upon the advantages to the child of a method whereby she "learns by doing". They did not, however, continue to support the original Froebelian plays with the toys or Gifts, the art handwork or the singing games and plays.[11]

---

[9] S. J. Curtis, *History of Education in Great Britain*, London: University Tutorial Press Ltd., 1961, p. 298.

[10] Evelyn Lawrence (ed.) *Friedrich Froebel and English Education*, London: University of London Press Ltd., 1952, p.91.

[11] *Ibid.*, p. 13.

The second development which influenced infant education in Britain was the work of Maria Montessori. Dr. Montessori had designed apparatus which utilized the child's senses in the learning process. The apparatus included geometric insets, sandpaper letters and numbers and frames for lacing and buttoning. The letters and numbers were used to teach the three R's. The apparatus met with instant approval when it was introduced into some of the infant schools.

About this time there was a growing feeling among teachers in Britain that a child should be given more freedom. Educators felt this would be possible using the Montessori apparatus because a child could work with it independently. Furthermore, stationary furniture was replaced by moveable furniture adapted in size to the small child. This also gave the child a greater degree of independence.[12]

The third development in Britain was the Nursery School Movement. This movement owed its existence to the efforts of Rachel and Margaret McMillan. These two sisters were originally concerned about the health and welfare of small children, especially those who lived in the crowded industrial cities of Britain. They first opened health clinics for children under the age of five. Their concern met a vital need, for, from 1905 on, local education authorities were no longer required to admit children under five into the infant

schools. Then, in 1911, the McMillan sisters opened their first nursery school in Britain for children aged two to five at Deptford.

The program for their school was similar to the programs of present-day nursery schools. When a child arrived in the morning she underwent a rapid medical inspection for the detection of any signs of illness or disease. During the day she played outdoors, at noon ate a hot meal and then in the afternoon rested on a cot.

By the *Education Act* of 1918, Local Education Authorities in England were empowered to establish nursery schools. The Board of Education offered grants toward the establishment of such schools from 1919 onward. However, it was not until the *Butler Act* of 1944 that Local Education Authorities were urged by the newly-created Ministry of Education to take advantage of the grants offered and provide either nursery schools or nursery classes in existing schools for children under the age of five, the age of compulsory school attendance in Britain.

Thus, the Child Study Movement, the Montessori System and the Nursery School Movement helped to modify and change programs in the British infant schools. More large muscle activity was introduced, the children were given greater freedom and more attention was paid to a child's physical health. Over the years psychologists such as Susan Isaacs have helped to clarify issues relating to both program and methodology and the Nursery School Movement has made

---

[12]*Ibid.*, p. 92.

further contributions. All of these factors combined to focus attention on the need for popular education to extend downward and include the three and four-year-old child.

Early Childhood Education in the United States

In 1854, Henry Barnard, founder and editor of the *American Journal of Education*, and later the first Commissioner of Education in the United States, attended the Exhibition of the Royal Society of Arts in London. There he saw the Froebelian kindergarten display of Baroness von Marenholtz-Bülow and then visited Madame Ronge's kindergarten. Impressed by what he saw and heard, he gave support to the Froebelian Kindergarten Movement when he returned to the United States. According to Neith Headley, the first article about the kindergarten to appear in an American journal was written by Henry Barnard. In it, Barnard told of his visit to the London Exhibit.[13].

Dr. Barnard's support of the Froebelian kindergarten could not but help further its cause. James L. Hughes of Toronto claimed he was "the first man to decide the kindergarten should be an organic part of the free state school systems of the world"[14]

This was a significant claim in view of the fact that in 1836 in Connecticut, Dr. Barnard had promoted the first free-school law in the world.

Private kindergartens which were opened in various parts of the United States received enthusiastic, albeit small, support. Among the supporters none was more eager than Elizabeth Peabody of Boston. In her enthusiasm she traveled to Europe to see the Froebelian kindergarten for herself. While there, she encouraged educators trained in Froebelian theory and practice to emigrate to the United States.

In America Elizabeth Peabody did much to make the Froebelian kindergarten known. She lectured on Froebelianism and undertook the publication of a kindergarten journal. Together with her sister, Mary Mann, Elizabeth Peabody compiled a guide book for kindergarten educators.[15] In 1870, she organized the first free kindergarten in America, supported by private donations. Then, in 1877, she helped to found the American Froebel Union. Included among its charter members were Dr. Henry Barnard; Dr. William T. Harris; Dr. William N. Hailmann; Professor John Kraus and

---

Kindergarten Union, New York: The Century Co., 1924, p. 65.

[15]Mrs. Horace Mann and Elizabeth P. Peabody, *Moral Culture of Infancy and Kindergarten Guide*, New York: J. W. Schemerhorn and Co., 1869. Mary Mann was the widow of Horace Mann who is remembered as the Father of American Public Education.

---

[13]Neith Headley, *op. cit.*, p. 11.

[14]James L. Hughes, "Personal Recollections of Henry Barnard." *Pioneers of the Kindergarten in America.* Prepared by the Committee of Nineteen of the International

his wife, Maria Kraus-Boelte; as well as Elizabeth Peabody's sister, Mary Mann.

The first kindergarten to be opened as part of the public school system was in St. Louis, Missouri, in 1873. It was introduced into the public schools by William T. Harris, then Superintendent of Schools in St. Louis, but later the Federal Commissioner of Education in Washington, D.C., and Susan E. Blow, who became well known in the United States for her advocacy of the Froebelian kindergarten. Dr. Harris was familiar with the writings of Froebel, Pestalozzi and Herbart as well as those of Georg Wilhelm Friedrich Hegel (1770-1831) and other German idealist philosophers.

Susan Blow received her kindergarten training in 1872 from Madame Kraus-Boelte, who had recently arrived in New York and opened a kindergartner's training class.[16] As well as working towards the establishment of the kindergarten in St. Louis, Susan Blow lectured on various aspects of the Froebelian kindergarten and wrote several books on kindergarten education. These were also read and studied by educators in Ontario. In her lifetime she became known as the North American philosopher of the Froebelian kindergarten.

The public school kindergarten in St. Louis was Froebelian in that it was based on Froebelian principles and practices, but it had certain distinguishing characteristics. It was for children aged four to six. The half-day session was usually held in the morning. There could be as many as 75 children in a kindergarten room. They were guided in their education by a director, her paid assistants[17] and the unpaid student assistants.

In contrast, Froebel's kindergarten was for children aged three to seven and they attended all day. In fact, his kindergarten was residential for some children, certainly for his nephews. Numbers of children in Froebel's kindergarten ranged between 12 and 24. That the St. Louis kindergarten differed from Froebel's kindergarten in these practical ways no doubt limited the extent to which Froebelian principles and practices could be fully realized.

Maria Kraus-Boelte (1836-1918) was very much concerned that the true Froebelian kindergarten education be understood. She had studied with Froebel's widow in Hamburg, Germany,[18] and then for a

---

[16]Trainees in the Froebel system were referred to as *kindergartners* or *child nurturers*.

[17]It was usual to have a director and an assistant for 60 children. Another assistant was hired for approximately every 30 children.

[18]It was reported that when Frau Froebel saw Maria Boelte's work, she exclaimed, "Oh, that Froebel had known you! . . . You are, in truth, his spiritual daughter!" (*Pioneers of the Kindergarten in America*, p. 79).

short time had assisted Madame Ronge in the kindergarten in London, England. In 1872, she emigrated to New York where she opened a private kindergarten, started a mothers' class and began to train kindergarten educators. In 1873, she married John Kraus and together they wrote *The Kindergarten Guide* which was comprised of two volumes.[19] Maria Kraus-Boelte not only provided training for Susan Blow of St. Louis, but also for Ontario's first Kindergarten Director, Ada Marean, who later became Mrs. James L. Hughes of Toronto. Both Dr. and Mrs. Hughes had only praise for Madame Kraus-Boelte. At the time of the celebration of her fiftieth anniversary in kindergarten work, James L. Hughes paid her high tribute in a letter he wrote.

> In my opinion no other leader in any country since the time of Froebel has had so clear a vision as you have had of the great fundamental principles underlying the highest development of humanity, and of their relationship to each other.[20]

However, in spite of the enthusiastic support which the kindergarten received in the United States, it encountered many difficulties. There was always criticism from those who did not understand the child development emphasis in the kindergarten or Froebel's suggested method of education, play. But by far the most serious situation the American Kindergarten Movement had to face was a schism which divided its own members. The schism, which began during the 1890's and lasted for some twenty years, divided the Movement into two camps - the Froebelians on one side and the Reconstructionists, the name they adopted, on the other.[21] Susan Blow became the champion of the Froebelians and Patty Smith Hill of Louisville, Kentucky, emerged as the champion of the Reconstructionists. At the time, Ontario was not involved in the controversy but, because the outcome did influence the kindergarten in Ontario at a later date, it is worthwhile to be aware of the issues involved in the American schism.

The Reconstructionists advocated changes in the kindergarten based on the psychological findings of child study, as well as upon the educational views of John Dewey. In the mid-1890's, Professor Hall and Patty Smith Hill were two of the first educators to advocate a critical analysis of the traditional Froebelian

---

[19] Maria Kraus-Boelte and John Kraus, *The Kindergarten Guide* , 2 Vols.; New York: E. Steiger & Co., 1882, 1889.

[20] Pamphlet, courtesy of Laura Hughes Lunde, daughter of James L. Hughes and Ada Marean Hughes, "Maria Kraus-Boelte, in Celebration of Fifty Years of Kindergarten Work - An Account of the Reception held in New York, December 2, 1909 at the Hotel San Remo," p. 12.

---

[21] Patty Smith Hill, *Kindergarten,* A reprint from the *American Educator Encyclopedia,* Washington: Association for Childhood Education 1942, p. 1962.

kindergarten. In retrospect, once their changes had been effected, Patty Smith Hill credited Professor Hall with much of the reorganization of the kindergarten, but she claimed it was John Dewey who had transformed both the kindergarten and the primary school in the United States.[22] Certainly, as education students who had been taught by both Hall or Dewey graduated and entered the teaching profession, the position of the Reconstructionists grew stronger. The criticisms of the Froebelian kindergarten which were raised by supporters of the Child Study Movement in Britain have already been discussed. Therefore, at this juncture, reference will be made only to Dewey's views on education, views that were destined to have a profound effect not only upon the American kindergarten but upon all American education.

John Dewey (1859-1952) was a young man when enthusiasm for the New Education was at its height in the United States. He, too, came under the influence of Rousseau, Pestalozzi and Froebel, but particularly of Herbart, although he later disassociated himself from the Herbartians. He was also at one time a student of Professor Hall's. Dewey came to a position where he rejected any theory of education which suggested aims but offered no realistic means of achieving them. However, he did advocate and forward the method suggested in the New Education, that a child should learn through her own activity.

Dewey's co-worker was William Heard Kilpatrick, the exponent of the Project Method. The project began from an expression of the child's interest or need and was directed toward a desirable end. The project turned the classroom into what Dewey considered the best learning situation, a "busy workshop".[23]

Dewey believed life was a "continual readaptation of the environment to the needs of living organisms".[24] He believed that, for the human race to survive, man needed to learn how to adapt to his environment as well as how to adapt his environment to himself. To Dewey, readaptation should be made in such a way as to ensure the social progress of man. Therefore, education should be to train the child for social usefulness within her own environment, the school becoming a part of daily life, not remaining apart from life. The atmosphere within the school was to be one of freedom, freedom for a child to grow and develop within a framework of social co-operation. It was through activity that the child learned how to adapt to her environment and how to adapt it to herself.

The interrelationship of the physical and intellectual was important

---

[22]*Ibid.*, p. 1963.

[23]L. A. Pechstein and Frances Jenkins, *Psychology of the Kindergarten-Primary Child*, Boston; Houghton Mifflin Co., 1927, pp. 206-208.

[24]John Dewey, *Democracy and Education* , New York: The Macmillan Co., 1916, p. 2.

to Dewey. "The material of thinking is not thoughts, but actions, facts, events, and the relationship of things."[25] The intellectual life, however, was not without discipline. Within each experience, Dewey would encourage the child to develop the attitude of the scientific mind.

> The real problem of intellectual education is the transformation of natural powers into expert, tested powers: the transformation of more or less casual curiosity and sporadic suggestion into attitudes of alert, cautious and thorough inquiry.[26]

In summary, then, Dewey would train a child for social usefulness by planning experiences for her which required activity. These activities helped her to understand the environment and her role in it. Physical and intellectual freedom were necessary in order for the child to come to that understanding. In this way, Dewey hoped to develop within the child the true spirit of scientific inquiry. The Reconstructionists, in their desire to change the Froebelian kindergarten, emphasized two aspects of Dewey's thought, the socialized curriculum and the educational method of activity. They felt both could further the child's physical and intellectual growth.

Patty Hill, the spokesman for the Reconstructionists, concurred with both Hall and Dewey. She agreed with Dewey that the kindergarten should be a community of children and, therefore, that their activities should have as a primary purpose the benefit of the whole group. For example, when weaving, the child could make a rug for the doll house, or when sewing, make clothes for the family of dolls. She agreed with Dewey, as well, that discipline should be developed through the social co-operation of the children. Patty Hill, along with Professor Hall, objected to what they felt was a mystical significance of Froebel's equipment and materials. Froebel had designed his equipment and materials to correspond to fundamental forms in nature and according to laws of development which he saw as God's laws operating in nature. He believed these laws were best expressed mathematically. It was this symbolic interpretation of his equipment and materials which some tended to label as mystical. The Reconstructionists were also opposed to the smallness of the toys and the fine handwork required from the child, favouring large muscle activity instead.

Further, Patty Hill advocated free play within a structured environment in place of Froebel's singing games and plays which she believed restricted the child's movements. Although she did criticize so much in the Froebelian program, she agreed with the Froebelians that the

---

[25]*Ibid.*, p. 184.

[26]John Dewey, *How We Think*, Boston: D. C. Heath & Co., 1910, p. 62.

child was of utmost importance and learned best through her own activity.[27]

Susan Blow, who championed the Froebelian cause, answered many of the criticisms of the Reconstructionists in a book entitled *Educational Issues in the Kindergarten*..[28] In it she dealt with three issues: she compared the new "industrial" or socialized program with the Froebelian program, she discussed free play in the light of Froebel's guided plays and she contrasted the concentric program which was the correlation of subject matter with Froebel's views on self-activity.

Susan Blow argued that the socialized program was one-sided in its emphasis on the centrality of humankind. She believed, with Froebel, that the curriculum in the kindergarten should include a knowledge of God and of nature, as well as an understanding of people and the world shaped by humankind. She criticized the utilitarian aspects of a curriculum which required every activity to have a useful purpose. She feared the emphasis would shift from the process of development going on within the child to the results of the child's activity.

To Susan Blow, discipline was the development of self-control within

the child. A child who was created in the image of God bore the image of the Divine and could, therefore, be inspired by noble thoughts and good deeds. Blow urged kindergarten directors to place before the child such ideals of behaviour as kindness and industry. She also encouraged educators to nurture goodness in a child and not to permit any destructive qualities opportunity for growth. She agreed with the Reconstructionists, however, that the child could best develop self-control within a social setting.

In answer to the questions raised by the Child Study Movement, Blow pointed out that Froebel's curriculum provided for both the child's large and small muscle development. She claimed that the small Froebelian toys and materials were designed to develop the fine muscles of the hand, whereas the Froebelian plays, and more especially gardening, were to provide healthy exercise for a child's large muscles.

Susan Blow also discussed free play in the light of Froebel's guided plays. She claimed free play could prove to be aimless for a child and leave her development too much to chance. She noted that Froebel in his singing games had utilized the universal and traditional plays of childhood to further child development. Blow objected to free play because of the dangers she could foresee. She believed that if a child were continually allowed to follow her instincts in response to suggestions from the environment, that child would eventually become a slave to inner impulses.

---

[27]Patty Smith Hill, *Kindergarten*, p. 1965.

[28]Susan E. Blow, *Educational Issues in the Kindergarten*, New York: D. Appleton & Co., 1909.

By 1903, the schism which had developed in the Kindergarten Movement between the Froebelians and the Reconstructionists was serious enough to prompt the International Kindergarten Union to appoint a Committee to study the issues which divided them.[29] The Committee appointed by the Kindergarten Union became known as the Committee of Nineteen. In their report, which was published in 1913, three different views of kindergarten education were presented.[30] Patty Hill championed the point of view of the Reconstructionists and Susan Blow the position of the Froebelians, while the third section of the report was a brief moderate statement by Elizabeth Harrison who had studied with both Blow and Kraus-Boelte. Ada Hughes of Ontario, who was a member of the Committee of Nineteen, signed Blow's section of the report, indicating her support of the Froebelian kindergarten.

Faced, however, with the growing strength of the Reconstructionists, the Froebelians gave way. Although differences of opinion continued to exist, the breach healed quickly, possibly because both groups always kept the child in the forefront of their educational thinking. Froebel's doctrine of self-activity was continued in Dewey's thought with his emphasis upon the importance of the child's activity but the Froebelian program was discarded. Froebel's small toys were replaced by bigger objects and larger handwork materials were introduced. Both the toys and materials were added to and used in ways very different from Froebel's original plan. Finally, free play was accepted in place of Froebel's guided plays. The ideal American kindergarten became a miniature society where each activity served a useful purpose, and where each child learned self-control through social co-operation. Over the years, the changes in the American kindergarten have been sufficient to cause Neith Headley to write, "The modern Kindergarten, however, is a far cry from the early Froebelian Kindergarten."[31]

---

[29] The International Kindergarten Union was formed in 1892 in the United States. In 1930, it became part of a larger organization, the Association for Childhood Education.

[30] *The Kindergarten*, Reports of the Committee of Nineteen of the International Kindergarten Union on the Theory and Practice of the Kindergarten, Boston: Houghton Mifflin Co., 1913.

---

[31] Neith Headley, *op. cit.*, p. 3.

CHAPTER II

FRIEDRICH FROEBEL'S KINDERGARTEN

Metaphysics – Froebel's Doctrine of Unity

*F*roebel as a Christian believed that God was the Source of all things, the Creator of all things, and the Sustainer of all things by his Spirit, and that Jesus was the mediator between heaven and earth, between God and mankind. All things had their origin in God and the universe was an expression of the goodness of its Creator. Humankind was to live in harmony with him, with each other and to be stewards of his creation.

God had created the universe but he was still active in it, for the universe was still "becoming".[1] Creation implied force and force led to diversity. Even those things which appeared to be opposites were related at their source because God was the creator of all things. "We fail to see that every external separation implies an original inner unity," stated Froebel.[2] He referred to the concept of the harmony of all things as *the law of*

connection. It was his most significant law.[3]

Mankind was unique in God's creation because they alone were created in his image. Just as God was both active and creative, men and women were meant to be both active and creative. Their true essence was spiritual because God's spirit dwelt within.[4] God intended humanity to be filled with his life, love and light. Thus, it was possible for each person inwardly to develop a harmony of spirit, heart, mind and body, as well as outer relatedness with God, humankind and nature. Persons made in God's likeness had the capacity to comprehend and enjoy the harmony which he intended. When the child was yet an infant in the home, the love within the family circle revealed to him that harmony which was God's love.[5] Nurtured in the Christian faith, the child learned that Jesus had come to earth from heaven "in order that the sternest contradictions of life might be solved. . . ." Even in his play, the child would

---

[1] Friedrich Froebel, *Education by Development,* trans. Josephine Jarvis, New York:
D. Appleton & Co., 1902, p. 21.

[2] Friedrich Froebel, *The Education of Man,* trans. W. N. Hailmann, New York:
D. Appleton & Co. , 1907, p. 146.

[3] Froebel, *Education by Development*, p. 272.

[4] Friedrich Froebel, *Pedagogics of the Kindergarten*, trans. Josephine Jarvis, New York: D. Appleton & Co., 1900, pp. 7, 8.

[5] Friedrich Froebel's father was a Lutheran Minister. It was in accompanying his father on home visits that Froebel became aware of the damaging influence a home in conflict had on the children..

seek for this harmony in his inward life.[6]

Once the child became conscious of a harmony with God, he became more aware of all around him and gradually developed a clearer insight into the best use of his life. Full consciousness of himself as well as his environment was the way to freer self-development and a freer determining of his destiny, "for man is destined for consciousness, for freedom, and for self-determination".[7] It was the way, too, to a life of creative freedom.

> Mankind is meant to enjoy a degree of knowledge and insight, of energy and efficiency of which at present we have no conception; for who has fathomed the destiny of heaven-born mankind? But those things are to be developed in each individual, growing forth in each one in the vigor and might of youth, as newly created self-productions.[8]

One who failed to recognize God as his Creator gave no thought to his own spiritual well-being nor to that of his children. Froebel believed such a man could not fully understand God's universe. Failing to acknowledge God, he felt independent from him and thus never discovered the harmony of life for which God had created him. The man who did recognize and acknowledge God, however, discovered the harmony of life.

> He may rise to the highest knowledge, not alone of man, but of all created beings, to a knowledge of the truth that the infinite is revealed in the finite, the eternal in the temporal, the celestial in the terrestrial, the living in the dead, the divine in the human.[9]

God's laws, which were inherent in all things because He created and sustained all things, also, to Froebel, revealed the harmony in all of life. Man and nature alike were subject to these laws, but they could be observed more readily in nature than in man. Thus, Froebel referred to nature as the book of God and claimed that the study of nature would lead to insight into laws of growth and development for all living things, persons included.[10]

As God and nature evidenced unity, so also did man. He was created to live in harmony with God and thus with his family, his social community

---

[6]Friedrich Froebel, *Mottoes and Commentaries of Friedrich Froebel's Mother Play*, trans. Henrietta R. Eliot and Susan E. Blow, New York: D. Appleton & Co., 1908, pp. 219-221.

[7]Froebel, *The Education of Man*, p. 136.

[8]*Ibid.*, p. 233.

[9]*Ibid.*, p. 149,

[10]Froebel, *Education by Development*, p. 246.

and all mankind. His life was to develop harmoniously from the past, in the present and on into the future. His actions were to be in harmony with his thoughts and his desires, desires which reflected God's goodness. It became the responsibility of parents and educators to make the child consciously aware of this possible harmony in his life.[11]

Education to Froebel was both an art and a science, and as such it was to be clear in its aim, means and subject matter. An aim was useless if there was no way to make it a reality in life. Educators, therefore, needed to determine means as well as aims. "For means and aim, way and goal, lie always very close together. . . ."[12] Froebel had one aim in education,and that was to lead the child into harmony with God. "In a single word, recognizing him as implicitly the child of God, your devout aim will be so to educate him that he shall become actually the child of God."[13] The God-likeness was to be drawn out from within the child, leading to a productive life, the child growing in harmony with God, humankind and nature.

By education, then, the divine essence of man should be unfolded, brought out, lifted

into consciousness, and man himself raised into free, conscious obedience to the divine principle that lives in him, and to a free representation of this principle in his life.[14]

The aim could only be achieved by an appropriate means. Christianity, therefore, not only presented the true purpose of education but it revealed the method. The child, reflecting God's image in his self-activity and creativity, should be guided by parents and educators to express himself in these ways to the laws of growth and development.

Froebel's Concept of Child Development and the Curriculum

The laws which Froebel recognized in the universe also reflected a harmony of life for they implied order as well as activity and applied to all children. For example, although there were common characteristics among children, each child was unique and, like the rest of God's creation, expressed himself both in unity and diversity.

God's laws did not limit growth, but rather allowed each part of creation the freedom to develop according to its own nature. "It is the destiny and life-work of all things to unfold their essence," wrote Froebel.[15]

---

[11]Froebel, *The Education of Man*, pp. 15, 16.

[12]Froebel, *Education by Development*, p. 12.

[13]Froebel, *Mottoes and Commentaries. . . ,* p. 56.

[14]Froebel, *The Education of Man*, pp. 4, 5.

[15]*Ibid.*, pp. 1-2.

He recognized and utilized in education this important principle or law, that the child would develop from within himself and according to his own being. The context was love and harmony, for "God neither ingrafts nor inoculates. He *develops*. . . ."[16]

An education which *developed* the child implied that adults needed to comprehend the child's nature, if possible from birth. Parents had the first responsibility. They were to consider carefully the child's total life — its beginnings and all its relationships, small and insignificant though they be. In Froebel's scheme of education, the child should be treated for "what he is, what he has, and what he will become".[17]

Froebel, in emphasizing the unity of all things, felt that the child as an integral part of the ordered creation should live in close association with adults. When they were together, the child learned through imitation while the adults had an opportunity to observe him, to listen to him and to learn to understand him. Perhaps Froebel was considering these benefits to the child when he wrote, "Come, let us live with our children."[18] In any case, he implied more than to play with a child.[19] Then, too, he brought adults and children into a harmonious relationship when he formed and established the kindergarten.

The fundamental and living thought of humanity, "Come, let us live with our children," becomes, when manifested in action, an institution for fostering family life and for the cultivation of the life of the nation, and of mankind, through fostering the impulse to activity, investigation, and culture in man, in the child as a member of the family, of the nation, and of humanity; an institution for self-instruction, self-education, and self-cultivation of mankind, as well as for all-sided and therefore for individual cultivation of the same through play, creative self-activity, and spontaneous self-instruction . . . .[20]

Froebel's concept of child development profoundly influenced his curriculum. The child had a solid foundation upon which he could build in the harmony of love which he found in his family. Then, too, it was during

---

[16]*Ibid.*, p. 328.

[17]Froebel, *Pedagogics*. . . , p. 12.

[18]*Ibid.*, p. 6.

---

[19]Robert Rusk has translated the phrase to read, "Come let us live in sympathy with our children", in *A History of Infant Education*, 2nd ed. rev., London: University of London Press, Ltd., 1951, p. 61. In the Froebel Foundation we say, "Come, let us live in harmony with our children."

[20]Froebel, *Pedagogics*. . . , p. 6.

these early years that impressions were made upon him, impressions which would be the bases for all his understanding.

> Where will the coming man find an object of thought and feeling, of knowledge and skill, that does not have its tenderest rootlets in the years of childhood? What subject of future instruction and discipline does not germinate in childhood?[21]

Educators needed to realize "that each detail of his [the child's] experience will continue to influence his history with a power that augments as life proceeds."[22] He criticized the school for being outside the life of the child and for teaching remote things which would not attract the children.

The curriculum was to awaken and nurture the heart, soul, mind and body of the child and at the same time continue to harmonize his relationships with God, humankind and nature. It included Christianity, physical health, training of the five senses, games and finger plays, gardening and the care of pets, language, literature, and dramatization, mathematics, and the use of equipment and materials, the Gifts and Art Occupations, which Froebel had designed in order to help the child

form accu_____ his wor_____ drawing, _____ they were _____ aid the _____ development. Froebel planned the curriculum in accord with laws of development so that the curriculum would develop with the child and at the same time serve to develop the child. Froebel referred to the relationship between the child and the curriculum in this way when speaking of his plays.

> They [the plays] continue to unfold in the progressive course of the development and education of the child in a logical sequence; and yet, as it were in harmony with the growth of the child, and unfold themselves anew and generate new things from themselves in their use, in their application, and in a manner suited to the course and the then existing stage of the child's development.[23]

This harmony of child and curriculum, the harmony of the psychological and logical, was a very important aspect of Froebel's kindergarten.

Emotional and Spiritual Development

In Froebel's understanding, living forms grew from within outwardly. "Whatever develops, be it into flower or tree or man, is from the

---

[21] Froebel, *The Education of Man,* pp. 83, 84.

[22] Froebel, *Mottoes and Commentaries. . . ,* p. 61.

[23] Froebel, *Pedagogics. . . ,* p. 146.

beginning implicitly that which it has the power to become."[24] A cultivated development starting from within the child made possible his fullest development. It began with the nurture of his heart. A child growing up in an atmosphere of love within the family found his emotional nature satisfied and nurtured. Educators were to build upon that development taking place within the home and continue to nurture his sympathies. In their loving concern for him they, too, would further his harmonious development .

It is not surprising, therefore, that Froebel said the Christian religion was to be taught both in the home and in the school.

> The school should first of all teach the religion of Christ; therefore, it should first of all, and above all, give instruction in the Christian religion; everywhere, and in all zones, the school should instruct for and in this religion.[25]

In the kindergarten, Christianity was not to take the form of dogmatic teaching, but rather the child was to experience God's love in social relations, to see God's pattern in nature and to live out God's goodness in kind deeds.

---

[24] Froebel, *Mottoes and Commentaries. . . ,* p. 68.

[25] Froebel, *The Education of Man,* p. 151.

Social Development

Mother-love was all important in the child's social development. The mother established the pattern in the child, for through her love she revealed the love of God to him and brought the child into relationships with the other members of the family. The parental love the child received in his home would later be given to others as he took his responsible place in society. Such a child brought to the kindergarten good social attitudes. In the social experience of the kindergarten, he would continue to be conscious of his individuality and yet become a member of the group and learn to see his possible contributions to that group. Therefore, the kindergarten provided a wider social sphere than it was possible for the family to give.

Physical Development

It was important to Froebel that the child's health was protected because a healthy physique aided child development. Activity served to strengthen the body, the child enjoyed it and activity brought him into contact with his environment. An alert adult could help the child understand his experiences and observations and relate them one to another and to himself. Physical activity, therefore, was important to inner growth and development.

True seeing involved the physical sense and a spiritual

perception. The door to the inner[26] development of mind, spirit and heart was the five senses of sight, hearing, touch, taste and smell;[27] the hand, the mediator between the inner child and his world. Knowledge gained in such a way was transformed by the child's thoughts and feelings. Through the senses he could learn to read the language of things. It was more than a knowledge of form, properties or relationships because it included understanding of the right and proper use of things.

> He who truly cultivates his senses and is then pliant to their suggestions will learn through them to recognize the true nature of sense-objects, and will avoid on the one hand injury to his health, and on the other the necessity of destroying the sense-object in order to get enjoyment out of it.[28]

It was difficult to determine when the physical sensation ceased and spiritual insight began, causing the child to understand the deeper significance of things. Therefore, it was important that the child's senses receive proper attention. "In sensation the physical and psychical, the merely

vital and the intellectual, the instinctive and the moral, melt into each other. Hence the importance of sense culture."[29] Froebel lamented a world "where the cultivation of the outer sensual eye is still so far in advance of the cultivation of the inner spiritual eye. . . ."[30]

To further promote education through the child's physical activity, Froebel invented games and plays, among them the finger plays. Their purpose, in part, was to develop the fine motor co-ordination of the child's hands. They also opened to him new conceptions and gave him much pleasure. For example, in the play, "Naming the Fingers", a suggestion was left with the child that he should know how to use his hands in worthwhile labour and in doing kind deeds for others.[31] Another finger play offers a very different idea. In "The Shadow Rabbit", shadow pictures were cast on the wall when the hands and fingers were manipulated in front of a light. It was the light that made the play possible. Froebel would have the child understand that God's love and light transformed life's dark experiences.[32]

---

[26]Where reference is made to the *inner* child it refers to his mind, spirit and heart; in contrast to what is outward, which is the physical.

[27]Froebel, *Mottoes and Commentaries. . . ,* p. 90.

[28]*Ibid.*, p. 92.

---

[29]Froebel, *Mottoes and Commentaries. . . ,* p. 96.

[30]Froebel, *The Education of Man,* p. 148.

[31]Froebel, *Mottoes and Commentaries. . . ,* p. 147.

[32]*Ibid.*, pp. 195, 196.

There were always these deeper meanings in Froebel's plays.

Games and Plays

Froebel planned his games and plays to further aid the child's "progressive" development.[33] The plays were universal ones but the child was given freedom within them, according to the natural laws, to develop in his own way. The plays developed one from another, yet always suited to the child's level of development and providing him with a challenge. They progressed from the familiar to the unfamiliar, the simple to the complex and the visible to the invisible but always returned to the familiar, simple and visible. They required of the child physical movement, emotional expression and control, social response, language, intellectual effort and the capacity to recognize spiritual truths.

> They are in general, therefore, the plays of observations, comparison, and consequently apperception; plays for the exercise of thought, for the fostering, development and cultivation of the reason, the intellect, the head and heart, manners, and modesty, as well as of morality and the highest union of life — the greatest

fostering and observation of life in all relations.[34]

The plays were divided into Movement Plays and Representation Plays. The Movement Plays, which brought the child into contact with his world, involved walking, running and the development of skills. What Froebel termed "journeys of discovery" were excursions into the community where the child would become familiar with the adult world.[35] In the swinging plays, the child imitated the pendulum movements discovered in play with the Gifts. The second group of plays, the Representation Plays, provided for the ethical and moral development of the child. In the singing games he imitated life in nature as well as social and cultural life. Physical action, intellectual understanding and spiritual truth were united within the child in these plays by word, gesture and song.

All the games began with the children in a circle which gave them an impression of unity in the play. Each child was to have a turn as leader so that each would be aware of himself as an individual and yet as part of the group. The plays were always accompanied by songs and stories which helped the child relate the activities and discoveries to himself.

---

[33] Froebel, *Education by Development,* pp. 261, 262.

[34] *Ibid.,* p. 345.

[35] Froebel, *Pedagogics. . . ,* p. 244.

Nature

The child's physical activities also brought him into contact with the things of nature from which he received impressions of his world. The kindergartner who accompanied the child on these excursions helped him to learn the names of seeds, plants and animals. In her use of language and song she helped him to understand nature's ways, to see relationships and to develop an awareness of space, time and seasons.

In gardening and by caring for pets the child learned to give nurture. He tended them but depended upon God for their life and growth. Froebel inquired, "What is the supreme gift you would bestow on your children who are the life of your life, the soul of your soul?"[36] He answered his own question, "Would you not above all other things render them capable of giving nurture? Would you not endow them with the courage and constancy which the ability to give nurture implies?"[37] If it was impossible to have a garden, the child planted seeds in a windowbox. Froebel also used seeds, pebbles, fruits and vegetables to make toys for the child, calling them "Gifts".

Language Development

Froebel ranked language development equally with religion and nature study. He defined it as the "inner living connection of all things".[38] By means of language the child on one hand was aided in his understanding of the world and on the other he was enabled to express his thoughts and feelings.

To Froebel, language was the outcome of a thinking mind, yet a child needed guidance to develop vocabulary, understand meanings and to know how to use language. This is why Froebel advised the kindergartner to talk or sing to the child about all of his activities. In this way even chance activities became clear to him.

Froebel suggested various types of stories be used. Recognizing that an adult could not devote all of his or her time to a particular child, he would have the parent say, "See all you can, so that you may have much to tell me... ."[39] Then, when the child spoke about his activities, the parent wove them into a story in order to bring the child's varied experiences into relation with each other. Children also enjoyed stories of special events, everyday life and nature, as well as fairytales and legends. Froebel believed the latter two revealed the mystery of life to the child, making him aware that there were events and occurrences in life which he would not understand.

---

[36] Froebel, *Mottoes and Commentaries. . .*, p. 229.

[37] *Ibid.*

[38] Froebel, *The Education of Man*, p. 209.

[39] Froebel, *Mottoes and Commentaries. . .*, p. 145.

Language development was also important in helping the child express himself. He needed to be aware of his individuality within the social group in order to become conscious of the fact that he had thoughts of his own which he could and should express. Dramatization was another form of self-expression as was printing .

Learning to read opened out exciting and challenging possibilities for the child. Froebel described how Lena, a six-year-old child in the kindergarten (his kindergarten, remember, was for children ages three to seven) learned how to print and then to read. She began by printing her own name, but only after she had practised outlining it in capital letters with the sticks of the eighth Gift. Next she learned to outline and print the names of her family members. She also learned the sound of each letter as she used it. Finally, she wrote a letter to her father who happened to be away from home on business at the time. For a long time she had longed to be able to write to her father when he was away. Her father was very pleased with her letter and gave her much encouragement.

Lena's interest in the alphabet and words also stimulated her enjoyment of picture books, so all of these activities combined to make printing and reading meaningful for her. What was significant to Froebel was that printing and reading began

because they met an inner need within Lena.[40]

> Now since reading and writing are of such great importance to man, the boy (when he begins to practice them) should possess a sufficient amount of strength and insight. The possibility of self-consciousness must have been developed in him; the inner need and desire to know them must have manifested itself clearly and definitely, before he begins to learn these arts.
> If he is to learn these arts in a truly profitable way, the boy must himself already have become something of which he can become self-conscious, instead of labouring to become conscious of what he has not yet come to be; otherwise, all his knowledge will be hollow, dead, empty, extraneous, mechanical.[41]

Intellectual Development

The intellect was to be developed in relation to the child's heart and feelings, for such a foundation would never become dead or mechanical. In developing the thinking child, educators encouraged him to use concrete objects creatively. Thus, through activity, impressions were gained by the child through his five

---

[40] Froebel, *Pedagogies. . .*, p. 287.

[41] Froebel, *The Education of Man*, p. 225.

senses. Understanding was developed as the adult added language and song to the child's experience. The impressions gained from these concrete experiences were the hidden beginnings upon which subsequent learning would be built. Later, when the child had a sufficient background, pictures and symbols could be used.

> If, therefore, you wish your instruction to be natural and impressive, begin by giving concrete experiences. Do you ask why this method is impressive and why its results are abiding? I answer: That which we have ourselves experienced makes a deep impression; for in experience three things are always present; the particular fact, its universal implication, and the relationship of both to the person who has the experience.[42]

It was in accord with Froebel's philosophy that the child learned to recognize the harmony of all things. Experiences provided for the child were to be related to each other as well as appropriate for the child's development. The essential business of the adult was to help the child relate his experiences one to another and to himself. By so doing the adult would help the child to see life as a connected process.

> Only that has real existence for man which has passed in and by

clear consciousness, which, as it were, had been born anew in spirit, and indeed. . . was recognized not as merely isolated but as an active member of a greater whole.[43]

Froebel referred to the mystery of knowledge. He said it became "more and more precise, and at the same time more and more manifold".[44] The simple developed into the complex, the near into the far. Froebel would have the child, then, progress from the simple to the complex, the known to the unknown. However, the child was always returned to the simple and the known that he might view each object or experience as a unit. This principle of relationship was very important in all the kindergarten activities.

Mathematics

To Froebel, mathematics was the mediator between thought and one's perception of nature.[45] Human beings and nature alike were subject to God's laws which were laws or principles of both unity and diversity. By using mathematics it was possible to trace those laws in the universe. Mathematics could reveal characteristics

---

[42] Froebel, *Mottoes and Commentaries. . . ,* p. 122.

[43] Froebel, *Education by Development,* p. 164.

[44] *Ibid.,* p. 259.

[45] Froebel, *The Education of Man,* pp. 204, 205.

of both the material world and invisible phenomena, ideas such as dimension, space, order, and rhythm. Furthermore, it could be used to calculate energy and force. Mathematics was and is a dynamic study and Froebel felt it should be presented in such a way to the child.

Rhythm, too, provided a basis for the teaching of mathematics. To Froebel, each child had an innate sense of rhythm. Furthermore, God's rhythm could be seen in nature with its division of time; the rhythm of the seasons, day and night, and hours and minutes. The concepts of long and short were also important to a child's understanding of time and rhythm. Thus, Froebel suggested the adult say to the child, "You must work now, but only for a short time . . ."[46] and be prepared to give the child that exact experience.

Froebel designed his Gifts and planned the Art Occupations in part to give the child mathematical experiences with form, size and number. He considered numerals in themselves as empty and meaningless. His emphasis was always on thought leading to experience and, as well, thought growing out of experience.

Music and Art

Music and art were major parts of Froebel's kindergarten. Both were

outer expressions of the inner child, and revealed his inner being. Thus, both were truly creative activities.

Froebel had suggested that language be used to accompany a child's activities but words put to music were even better, for they not only stimulated the mind but the songs stirred the child's emotions. In song, the words passed through the child's mind into his heart and soul.

A child was full of music and rhythm, but he needed opportunities to express what was within him through rhythmic movement and speech as well as song. Froebel devised his singing games because he was aware of the delightful influence music had on the child's play. There were also songs to accompany the activities with the Gifts and Art Occupations. Some examples of the titles of his songs were the "Carpenter", "Tick! Tock!", and "The Little Gardener".[47]

Art was another means of nurturing inner development. Heart and feelings could be united in observing a lovely picture. Then, too, the child also learned forms of beauty as he made symmetrical designs as he played. Freer drawings, which were drawings of objects, were called by Froebel "forms of life". He suggested a child would enjoy the freedom and movement of drawing outlines in the

---

[46] Froebel, *Mottoes and Commentaries. . . ,* pp. 237, 238.

[47] Friedrich Froebel, *The Songs and Music of Friedrich Froebel's Mother Play,* prepared and arranged by Susan E. Blow, New York: D. Appleton and Co., 1895.

air. He also pointed out that drawing, because it was representation by line, connected modelling which was a solid, with painting which was a surface, His suggestions for art work were embodied in the materials of the Art Occupations (*infra*, pp. 35-7).

Drawing which was a creative expression, also helped the child to understand his environment. He needed to learn how to observe before he could begin to draw. It required from him thoughtful comparisons and perception. "What man tries to represent or do he begins to understand," wrote Froebel.[48] Art was also a spiritual experience, for in the exercise of his creative power the child was drawn closer to the Creator.

Froebel knew that not every child would become an artist any more than every child would become a musician. Nevertheless, he believed each child should have opportunities for appreciation and enjoyment of both music and art.

Froebel's View of Creativity

Froebel's understanding of creativity was that the child was creative because everyone was made in the likeness of God, the Creator. God, by his Spirit, expressed Himself in self-active, creative energy in life, love and light – life in nature, love shared amongst persons and the light of wisdom. Through a study of nature,

the child could best see God's creative power but he also needed to realize himself to be a child of God, thus part of all humankind, and subject to the same laws as seen in nature.

Froebel likened the relationship of God to nature as that of an artist to his art. As art was an expression of the artist, so nature was God's expression. Therefore, as the artist's spirit could be discerned in his art, so God's creative spirit could be discerned in nature.

> Now, as the work of man, of the artist, carries within itself the *spirit* and *character*, the *life* and *essential being*, of this man, and – as we say in human metaphor exhaustively and most significantly – breathes out this spirit and life, and as the human being who produced it, who created it, as it were, out of himself, nevertheless remains the same undiminished and undivided being, and is even strengthened in his power by this work, thus, too, the spirit and being of God – although the cause and source of all existing things, and although all things carry within themselves and breathe the one spirit of God – remain nevertheless in themselves the one Being, the one Spirit, undiminished and undivided.[49]

It was God's Spirit within him that made the child creative and Froebel

---

[48]Froebel, *The Education of Man*, p. 76.

[49]*Ibid.*, p. 154.

believed all children naturally possessed "the all-quickening, creative power of child-life."[50] However, the child needed freedom to be active, freedom to be creative, freedom to unfold naturally according to principles operating in the universe and freedom to be and do what was right and good in God's image, for he, too, could express himself creatively in life, love and wisdom.

> The doing of what is good is the tie between Creator and creature. To do good with insight and intention makes the tie a conscious one. Therein is the living union of man and God – the union of individuals with God – the union of all humanity with God.[51]

It was through his self-activity that the child was able to express his inner creativity and thereby reveal his God-likeness. Through self-activity the child gave form to thought. In translating a thought into a deed, he made the invisible visible which was what God had done in the creation of nature. His thought-world was the world within himself and he strove, albeit in simple ways, to recreate his world. It was by striving that the child revealed himself as creative and through his productivity and creativity showed his resemblance to the Creator.

The child's choice of materials also satisfied the creative impulse. He might choose from the materials of nature – light, air, water, earth or even dust. The creative act began in the heart and mind but was expressed in a deed, whatever form that deed might take. Froebel was very anxious that the child be encouraged to make presents for those he loved. A present was possibly the most complete creative expression of the child because it involved heart, soul and mind, as well as physical skill.

Through his own creative expression and productive activity, the child gained a better understanding of his Creator. "He who would know the Creator must exercise his own creative power," claimed Froebel.[52] He must know himself to be both created and creative.

Froebel urged parents and educators to view the child as a creative being, to see him as God's child and to develop him in harmony with God. Creativity was a characteristic of the child but he would need from parents and educators both freedom and encouragement to become creative.

> The things a child can make
> May crude and worthless be;
> It is his *impulse to create*
> Should gladden thee![53]

---

[50]*Ibid.*, p. 89.

[51]Froebel, *Mottoes and Commentaries. . . ,* p. 275.

[52]*Ibid.*, p. 275.

[53]*Ibid.*, p. 273.

Froebel's Method

To Froebel aims and means were equally important. His aim in education was that the child know God and grow in harmony with him, humankind and nature. In knowing him the child would reflect God's image, which meant that the child would express himself in energy in terms of his creativity and self-activity. God was love and all that he did was good. Thus, the child should act out of a caring heart so that all his deeds, too, would be kind and good. Striving and doing were essential to the child's growth. The responsibility of the educator was to guide the child in his activity and that activity was play. Therefore, Froebel's method of kindergarten education was to guide the young child in his play.

The name "kindergarten" is also indicative of Froebel's method. In 1836, when he first had established his institution at Blankenburg, he called it a *Kleinkinderbeschäftigungsanstalt,* which, freely translated, meant "an institution where small children were occupied". Barop, the nephew of a co-worker of Froebel's, tells of being with him when he decided upon the name "kindergarten".

When Friedrich Froebel came back from Berlin, the idea of an institution for the education of little children had fully taken shape in his mind. I took rooms for him in the neighbouring Blankenburg. Long did he rack his brains for a suitable name for his new scheme. Middendorf and I were one day walking to Blankenburg with him over the Steiger Pass. He kept on repeating, "Oh, if I would only think of a suitable name for my youngest born!" Blankenburg lay at our feet and he walked moodily towards it. Suddenly he stood still as if fettered fast to the spot, and his eyes assumed a wonderful, almost refulgent, brilliancy. Then he shouted to the mountains so that it echoed to the four winds of heaven, "Eureka! I have it! KINDERGARTEN shall be the name of the new Institution!"[54]

The kindergarten to Froebel was a garden of children.[55] He believed children developed in the same way all living things develop, from within outwardly and as a result of their own effort. However, both children and plants need protection and guidance. Therefore, as a plant grows into what it has the potential to become when tended by a gardener, so a child through his self-activity becomes what he is to be under the watchful guidance of parents and educators. Those who guided children in Froebel's

---

[54]Friedrich Froebel, *Autobiography of Friedrich Froebel*, trans. Emilie Michaelis and H. Keatley Moore, New York: C. W. Bardun, Pub., 1889, p. 137.

[55]Froebel's concept of the kindergarten as a garden of children is not to be confused with the emphasis upon nature in his curriculum, where he wanted each child to plant and tend a garden (*supra*, "Nature", p. 24).

kindergarten, then, were called "kindergartners".

> It is the aim of our endeavor to make it possible for man freely and spontaneously to develop, to educate himself from his first advent on earth, as a whole human being, as a whole in himself, and in harmony and union with the life-whole – to make it possible for him to inform and instruct himself, to recognize himself thus as a definite member of the all-life, and, as such, freely and spontaneously to make himself known – freely and spontaneously to live.[56]

If the aim of education was harmony, then the atmosphere in which the child developed was to be a loving one. A child brought up in such an atmosphere never knew himself to be outside the love of God. Love was in all he knew and experienced of life. The atmosphere was also one of freedom in order to give the child opportunities to use all his powers. A child needed freedom to develop according to his own nature as well as freedom to seek his own experience. There was no stereotyped sameness to this development, for even children with a similar upbringing showed "a different individuality".[57] The responsibility of educators was to see that what the child needed was within his environment and their guidance protected him from harm and damaging influences. "Therefore," wrote Froebel, "education in instruction and training, originally and in its first principles, should necessarily be *passive, following* (only guarding and protecting), *not prescriptive, categorical, interfering.*"[58]

Play

> Play is the purest, most spiritual activity of man at this stage [the kindergarten age], and, at the same time, typical of human life as a whole – of the inner hidden natural life in man and all things. It gives, therefore, joy, freedom, contentment, inner and outer rest, peace with the world. It holds the sources of all that is good.[59]

Froebel would guide the child's play because he believed it to be the natural means for laying the foundation of a child's education and development. Play had deep significance for the child because it was an outer expression of his inner being. For example, Froebel, noticing that children enjoyed playing house, suggested they sensed in their play the sanctity of a happy home.

---

[56]Froebel, *Pedagogics. . .* , p. 9.

[57]Froebel, *Mottoes and Commentaries. . .* , p. 75.

[58]Froebel, *The Education of Man*, p. 7.

[59]*Ibid.*

Even play with dolls had deep significance.[60]

Play was also the mediator between the child and his world for through his play the child was able to harmonize his experiences. In play he very naturally incorporated new knowledge and skills. As he tested his plans and abilities in an attempt to master his environment, he began to know himself. The playing child was challenged to seek for what he did not know, sensing in a new experience something beyond himself. Thus, he sought after the unknown, the complex and the invisible. The child also understood that which he tried to do. Enjoying his plays over and over again, he made each experience his own.

All of Froebel's curriculum was planned to make use of the child's play: such activities as the Movement and Representation Plays, the songs and the Gifts and Art Occupations. His plays were suggestions to educators of how a child's own play could be used to further his development.

Not only *The Light-Bird* but all of the plays which precede and follow it have many meanings. Neither must it be supposed that the meaning suggested by me is, if not the *sole*, at least the highest one. My songs, mottoes, and commentaries are offered simply with the hope that they may aid you to

recognize and hold fast some part of what you yourself feel while playing these games, and to suggest to you how you may waken corresponding feelings in your child.[61]

The one essential feature of any play was its creativity, for the child's play was truly an expression of his inner being. Only a creative spirit could give the play life and meaning. Therefore, Froebel suggested many different ideas and materials which could be used for indoor and outdoor play.

The child imitated life in nature and society in his plays. He was encouraged to imitate whatever he noticed, for he seemed to learn easily by this approach. Froebel felt the child's tendency to imitate was well worth cultivating.

Rightly directed, it will lighten by more than half the work of education. Utilized at the proper stage of development, it will enable you to accomplish by a touch light as a feather what later you cannot do with a hundredweight of words.[62]

Responsibility was placed upon the adults to guide a child's attention to those things which were good for him

---

[60]Froebel, *Pedagogics. . .* , p. 93.

[61]Froebel, *Mottoes and Commentaries. . .* , pp. 189, 190.

[62]*Ibid.*, p. 227.

to imitate. For example, he enjoyed imitating adults at work and liked to be helpful. The "help" often caused more work for the adult, but it nurtured right attitudes in the child. There was no doubt in Froebel's mind that childhood was the time "when man is to be prepared for future industry, diligence, and productive activity".[63] He believed a child who played heartily would best be prepared for his life's work.

Guidance

A child needed adult guidance as he played; for one thing, he was developing lifelong habits. The adult was to accompany him and talk with him about his play, but be careful not to alter it directly or indirectly. If she were with him, she would know what things the child understood and what was not clear to him. From this, she would be able to plan experiences which would increase his understanding and clarify his impressions.

This individual guidance was possible when the kindergartner was responsible for twelve children.[64] If the kindergartner were not able to be with the child during his play, discussion afterward quickened the child's mind and perception, making the play more purposeful. Even when

he played alone, the child was never to play thoughtlessly or aimlessly. "In other words," wrote Froebel, "let us form such habits of attention that the child will never play without precisely grasping and comprehending inwardly what he has outwardly represented." [65]

Parents and educators were not to give the child answers, but place within his reach the means to discover answers for himself. What he discovered himself was more meaningful in his development than what he was told by others.

> To have found one fourth of the answer by his own effort is of more value and importance to the child than it is to half hear and half understand it in the words of another; for this causes mental indolence. Do not, therefore, always answer your children's questions at once and directly; but, *as soon as they have gathered sufficient strength and experience*, furnish them with the means to find the answers in the sphere of their own knowledge.[66]

Adults were also to encourage the child *to solve the problems he discovered* as he played. Life would no doubt hold difficulties for the child, so Froebel would have him learn to persevere in his play. The active child

---

[63]Froebel, *The Education of Man*, p. 34.

[64]Froebel, *Education by Development*, p. 224.

[65]Froebel, *Pedagogics. . .* , p. 176.

[66]Froebel, *The Education of Man*, pp. 86, 87.

was not to evade problems; rather, he was encouraged to seek out solutions. "In himself and through his own self-activity he must find the solution of all contradictions, the mediation of all apparently irreconcilable opposition."[67]

Although adults had such an important educative role in the life of the child, Froebel did not underestimate the ability of children to teach one another, although unconsciously, in their plays. He found children enjoyed the experience of learning from each other.

Responsibility was accepted as part of the play. Rules were to be just and fair and made clear to the child. Responsibility was truly a privilege, not a burden. Froebel found most children gladly accepted the responsibilities involved in their play. It was by accepting responsibility that they learned to live in accord with God's laws. Thus, they would develop habits and attitudes of fair play, loyalty, respect, kindness and justice.[68]

Froebel knew the active child would get into trouble because he would not foresee the consequences of his deeds. There were also children who simply behaved badly. However, Froebel claimed shortcomings in a child, for the most part, could be traced to a good quality which had been "repressed, misunderstood, or misguided",[69] or to instances where a child was either neglected or overindulged.[70]

For, surely, the nature of man is in itself good, and surely there are in man qualities and tendencies in themselves good. Man is by no means naturally bad nor has he originally bad or evil qualities and tendencies.... [71]

Humanity was created in the image of God, but one could fall short of God's plan. Badness was not a positive evil for it would not exist if there were no good to fall short of. To Froebel, the source of all evil was the claim that humanity could be independent from God. In failing to understand his relationship to God, one also might fail to comprehend God's laws in the universe, laws essential in understanding child development. Each person was created a self-active being in the likeness of his Creator, to be active in the doing of what was good. Failure to recognize such a purpose might result in a personal failure to find harmony in life.[72]

There was a way to avoid wrong activity, and that way was to provide the child with appropriate activity.

---

[67]Froebel, *Mottoes and Commentaries. . . ,* p. 221.

[68]Froebel, *Pedagogics . . . ,* pp. 86, 101.

[69]Froebel, *The Education of Man,* p. 121.

[70]Froebel, *Pedagogics . . . ,* p. 167.

[71]Froebel, *The Education of Man,* p. 120.

[72]*Ibid.,* pp. 120 -21.

Froebel's Equipment and Materials, The Gifts and Art Occupations

Froebel designed his play equipment and art materials according to the same principles involved in all of the kindergarten activities. They, too, were to develop the child in depth – physically, intellectually and spiritually – as well as to help him to understand God's world. The Gifts were concrete objects or toys which helped the child gain impressions of his world. The materials, the Art Occupations, gave the child opportunities for creative expression.

The first Gift consisted of six small soft balls with woollen covers of blue, green, yellow, orange, red and purple. A ball symbolized the unity of all things. The first Gift was given the infant to play with in the home. The second Gift - a wooden sphere, a cylinder and a cube - was for two- and three-year-old children.[73] The other Gifts were developed from the first two. The third and fifth were divisions of the cube and the fourth and sixth were brick-shaped. The third, fourth, fifth and sixth Gifts were used in the building plays. Froebel also spoke of a seventh and an eighth Gift which may have been further divisions of the cube and brick. Those who followed Froebel, however, made tablets the seventh Gift, sticks the eighth, points the ninth, and sticks and points for dimensional building, the tenth.

---

[73]Froebel, *Pedagogics* . . . , pp. 75, 102.

The Art Occupations were used in conjunction with the Gifts and gave the child further experiences with the ideas suggested in the Gifts. The Occupations included perforating, sewing, twining, braiding, paper cutting, weaving, paper folding and modelling. Play with seeds, pebbles and soaked peas gave the child experiences with points. Sticks, rings, twining and paper cutting made him familiar with lines. In sewing, the child united points and lines. Soaked peas and sticks were joined to form an outline. Weaving gave the child the experience of putting lines together to form a surface. Paper folding showed the child ways in which he could change surfaces. Solid objects were made of wax, loam or clay. In using the materials creatively, the child was learning to reshape his world and thus developing the capacity to one day determine his destiny. The emphasis was placed on the process of the child's activity rather than upon a finished article, but he was encouraged to make presents for those he loved.

The child gained impressions of his world as he played. Froebel believed the child would become familiar with fundamental forms in nature and, seeing a reflection of God's laws in his play with the Gifts and Occupations, come to a fuller understanding of realities in life. In writing about the Gifts, Froebel referred to *forms of knowledge, forms of beauty* and *forms of life*. Forms of knowledge were mainly mathematical concepts. Certainly, an emphasis was placed upon geometrical shapes. Forms of beauty were demonstrations of the laws of balance and proportion worked out in design. Life forms were representations of the familiar objects surrounding the child. Much of the symbolism in the Gifts and Occupations related to mathematics.

Froebel would have the child gain clear impressions not only of the outer appearance and shape of the Gifts but of their inner qualities. Froebel used the word *inner* with regard to the Gifts and other objects, to designate qualities which were not seen. For example, an *inner* quality of the ball was the axis. Therefore, language, expressed either in a creative story or song, was used in conjunction with the child's play. In this way his vocabulary was extended and he became more fluent in the use of language. Comparisons became clearer to him – above and below, soft and hard, or quiet and noisy. Froebel wrote, "Object and knowledge, perception and word, are yet in many ways as much united as body and soul".[74] It was through activity and language, then, that the child gained clear impressions, even though he would probably forget the words that were used.

Froebel's first Gifts were made of soft materials such as turnips, potatoes, cabbage stalks, soft wood and clay. These could be cut and their shapes changed so that the child might discover the inner qualities. A cube might be cut into layers to make surfaces or a surface divided into lines.[75] Part of the play was to break the Gifts apart and then put them together again by a different means such as twining or weaving. Froebel did not feel manufactured toys offered so many possibilities to the child as nature's basic materials. The Occupations provided the child with materials with which he creatively worked out his own ideas. To Froebel this "creative, formative activity" counteracted the tendency a child might have to be destructive.[76]

Froebel believed a child was freer in his creative expression if he had learned to be responsible in the care and use of his toys. Therefore, each Gift was kept in its own box rather than in a common receptacle. This helped the child learn to respect his toys as well as to develop a sense of order. The child placed the Gift box containing blocks upside-down on the table with the lid just slightly drawn out. Then, carefully, he drew the lid out all the way, heard the blocks fall and, lifting off the box, saw the cubes as a complete unit.[77] Froebel claimed that it was in seeing the cubes as a whole that the child unconsciously formed plans for using them. All of the cubes or bricks were to be used in the play. When the child had discovered and explored all of the possibilities of each Gift he might use two or more Gifts together.

---

[74]Froebel, *Education by Development*, p. 271.

[75]*Ibid.*, pp. 287, 343. The tablets and sticks were later used to illustrate surfaces and lines.

[76]*Ibid.*, p. 273.

[77] Froebel, *Pedagogics . . .* , pp. 123-24.

The Gifts and Art Occupations offered to the child equipment and materials that demanded of him activity and creative expression. They also challenged the child. They provided him with experiences that gave unity to word and deed, as well as harmony to his thinking and doing.

Thus life early receives for the child a significance, the child's intellect receives a material for thoughtful comparison, its [his] mind and heart the joyous feeling of satisfaction, its [his] body the strengthening feeling of ability. The senses receive certainty of perception; the members, especially the hands and fingers, adroitness of representation. You can see here in this little insignificant play, my dear reader, the effect which is the aim of the whole of the kindergarten as well as of these plays as a whole and also as an individual part – fitness for life and life union.[78]

Summary

Froebel, as a Christian, acknowledged God to be the author and finisher of all things as well as the sustaining power in the universe, and Jesus Christ as the mediator between heaven and earth. To Froebel, diversity suggested force and force implied an original unity which could be found alone in God. Froebel stressed the mediation of opposites and considered

the law of connection his most important law. Froebel's educational aim was to bring the child to God through love so that he would develop from within, and resemble God in the goodness and productivity of his self-activity and creativity. Thus, he would find the harmony in all of life.

Froebel, in his doctrine of unity, stressed the interdependence of humankind and nature upon God. In his kindergarten curriculum he provided for a harmonious development of the child in depth and at the same time in relation to God, persons and nature. Provision was made for the child's spiritual, emotional, social, physical and intellectual development. The curriculum included Christianity, games and plays (many of them concerned with human life and work as well as with nature), problem finding and solving, nature study and gardening, language, mathematics, music and art.

Froebel's method of education was to utilize the child's play, the self-activity of the young child. Through play the child's development was furthered and, at the same time, his impressions of the world were extended. It was important to Froebel that the child would discover relationships in his plays, both one to another and to himself. Each play was to be accompanied by language and song so that the child would form clear and accurate impressions. The child's experiences were always to coincide with his stage of development. In the beginning the educator would be a protector and guide. She was not to interfere with the child but neither was she to allow him to play aimlessly. She

---

[78]Froebel, *Education by Development*, p. 158.

was to nurture the good in the child and to plan further experiences whereby his impressions would be extended. Froebel likened her role to one of a gardener, hence the word "kindergartner".

Creativity was an important part of the child's self-activity. The child, in exercising his creative powers in love (relationships), light (knowledge and wisdom), and life (everyday affairs), developed in God-likeness and drew nearer to his Creator. To Froebel, the most complete creative expression of the child was for him to make a present for someone he loved.

Froebel designed equipment and materials called the Gifts and Occupations, based upon the same principles as all of his plays. The child gained impressions through his play and the kindergartner, by means of language and song, helped him to form clear and accurate ideas. The Art Occupations were materials the child used for creative expression, complementing the ideas presented in the Gifts. This, then, was the Froebel kindergarten that inspired educators in Ontario.

CHAPTER III

EARLY HISTORY OF THE FROEBELIAN KINDERGARTEN IN ONTARIO, 1883 TO 1913

E gerton Ryerson, Superintendent of Education for the Province of Ontario from 1844 to 1876, did much to prepare the way for the entrance of the Froebelian Kindergarten into Ontario. Just as Pestalozzi had prepared the way for the acceptance of Froebelian ideas in Europe, Britain and the United States, Pestalozzian ideas contained in Ryerson's Report of 1846, which Ryerson put into effect during his 30 years as Superintendent, prepared the Ontario system for the adoption of the Froebelian kindergarten.

Ryerson envisioned a unified school system which would be efficient, compulsory and free. He opposed sectarianism but he agreed with those who would make the Christian religion the basis of the school curriculum as well as its pervading principle. He also added more subjects to the curriculum including Pestalozzi's object lessons. Thus, by 1871, the Ontario system was ready to expand both downwards and upwards, as well as to become more diversified.

During the 1870's, graded schools appeared in the larger cities and classes were large. It was not unusual to have at least 50 children in a primary class. Large classes were part of the growth process in introducing universal education. In many cities, as well, children under the age of six were attending the primary classes in the schools.

In 1876, the American centennial year, a kindergarten display was organized at the Centennial Exhibition in Philadelphia by the Boston kindergartners, Maria Kraus-Boelte and others.[1] James L. Hughes, Inspector of Schools for Toronto, attended the Exhibition and was very impressed by the Froebelian kindergarten. On his way back to Toronto he stopped in New York to discuss kindergarten education with Maria Kraus-Boelte. With a view to the possible opening of a private kindergarten in Toronto, he asked her to recommend a kindergartner.

According to Lorne Pierce, who wrote a biography of Hughes while Hughes was still alive, this was not his first contact with the kindergarten. Two years earlier when in Boston on a visit to schools, he had noticed the enthusiasm of the daughter of the proprietor of a hotel where he was staying towards the school which she attended. The next day he visited her kindergarten and was introduced to a system of education designed to develop the whole child. On his return

---

[1]Paul V. McLaughlin, *The Froebelian Movement in the United States* (unpublished doctoral dissertation, University of Ottawa, 1952), p. 20.

to Toronto he began a lifelong study of the writings of Pestalozzi and Froebel.[2]

J. George Hodgins, at that time assistant to Egerton Ryerson and later Deputy Minister of Education,[3] also attended the American Centennial Exhibition and reported his impressions of the kindergarten display.

The KINDERGARTEN display for the purpose of practically showing kindergarten methods of instruction is exhibited. The school-room is simply but prettily fixed up, and has been the centre of attraction for large numbers of visitors. Miss Burritt, who is in charge, seems to have thoroughly mastered the system, and the readiness and dexterity with which her little pupils acquitted themselves have won the admiration of all who have seen them.[4]

Maria Kraus-Boelte recommended Ada Marean to Hughes as a kindergartner who would be well qualified to open a private kindergarten in Toronto. Ada Marean had studied with Kraus-Boelte in 1877 and had then become a kindergartner in Saint John, New Brunswick. Apparently Hughes contacted Marean, for she moved to Toronto and opened a private kindergarten in January of 1878.[5]

The kindergarten received enthusiastic support in Toronto. In August of 1879, Professor George Paxton Young of the University of Toronto addressed the Ontario Educational Association on the values of the kindergarten. He praised James Hughes for his efforts on its behalf.

Hughes continued to support the kindergarten in public lectures as well as by writing articles for various education journals. A number of articles in support of the kindergarten appeared in the *Canada School Journal*. At the time Hughes was a member of its editorial committee. In the column "Notes and News", it was suggested that the kindergarten would soon be introduced into the public school systems of Toronto, Stratford and London, and that courses for kindergartners would be offered in Normal Schools in both Toronto and Ottawa. The tone of the articles appearing in the *Journal* was always optimistic.

---

[2] Lorne Pierce, *Fifty Years of Public Service*, Toronto: Oxford University Press, 1924, pp. 89-91.

[3] J. George Hodgins was Deputy Minister of Education from 1876 to 1890.

[4] J. George Hodgins, *Special Report on the Ontario Educational Exhibition,* 1876, Toronto: Hunter, Rose & Co., 1877, p. 164.

---

[5] Word of mouth tradition holds that Kraus-Boelte recommended Ada Marean when James L. Hughes stopped in New York in 1876 to see her. This could not be correct. Ada Marean's notes from Kraus-Boelte's class were dated 1877. Kraus-Boelte would not likely recommend Marean as a kindergartner until after she had taken the kindergarten course.

The advisability of introducing the kindergarten into the lower departments of city and town schools has been favourably considered during the year in several parts of the Province of Ontario. It is almost certain that before the close of another year this delightful method will be firmly engrafted on our public school system. Private kindergartens are already in successful operation in the leading cities of the Dominion.[6]

The *Journal of Education*, edited by Egerton Ryerson, had included articles about Froebel's kindergarten as early as 1872.[7] In the various articles, child development in the kindergarten was likened to the care given plants by the gardener, for the children grew and developed within a pleasant kindergarten atmosphere. They were given proper guidance and the plays which were used furthered their education. The kindergarten was referred to as a community of children and these early years were called the "formative" years.[8]

Interest in the Froebelian kindergarten was kindled. By 1882,

the Honourable Adam Crooks, who was Minister of Education,[9] together with members of the Toronto School Board, decided to send James Hughes to St. Louis, Missouri, to investigate their public school kindergarten. Hughes was accompanied by a trustee of the Toronto Board. The report which they wrote as a result of their visit was included in both the *Report of the Minister of Education* for 1882 and the *Minutes of the Toronto School Board* for that same year.

Their report was divided into three sections. The first contained a brief statement of the purpose of the kindergarten; in the second, the kindergarten in St. Louis was described; and in the third section, suggestions were offered concerning the introduction of the kindergarten into Ontario. The stated purpose of the kindergarten in St. Louis was to further the development of children in harmony with God, man and nature through the child's own activity. St. Louis school officials who were very enthusiastic were quoted as saying that the kindergarten should be "the foundation of all Public School education".[10] Hughes and the trustee concluded their report by recommending that a kindergartner be chosen and a kindergarten started where other

---

[6]"Retrospect," *Canada School Journal,* II, June 1878, p 150.

[7]E. Taylor, "Two Hours in a Kindergarten," *Journal of Education for Ontario,* XXV (September 1872), p. 132.

[8]"The Kindergarten in Canada," *ibid.,* XXVIII (March 1875), pp. 39, 40

---

[9]The Honourable Adam Crooks became Minister of Education when Dr. Ryerson retired. He remained in office from 1876 to 1882.

[10]Ontario, *Report of the Minister of Education* (1882), p. 233.

teachers could be trained. They also recommended that Susan E. Blow and Clara Beeson Hubbard of St. Louis,[11] be invited to Toronto to give a series of lectures at the Normal School on various aspects of kindergarten education.[12] The outcome was that Blow and Hubbard came to Toronto in the fall of 1882 to speak to educators and, further, Ada Marean was sent to St. Louis to study the kindergarten system in preparation for its introduction into Toronto public schools.

Thus, the first public school kindergarten in Ontario was opened in January of 1883 at Louisa Street Public School in Toronto, with Ada Marean as the first Kindergarten Director. There were approximately eighty children enrolled. Marean was assisted by seven unpaid students who wished to become kindergartners.[13] At the same time she also started a mothers' class for the parents of the children who attended her kindergarten in order to try to bring into harmony each child's experiences both in the home and kindergarten.

Adaline Augusta Marean (1848-1929), who later became Mrs. James L. Hughes, was the pioneer kindergartner in Ontario. Her life was an example of vigour and accomplishment. Marean was born in the town of Maine, New York, and as a young woman attended the Albany Normal School. She taught for a short time in the community of California, Missouri, but in 1877, not satisfied with the teaching methods of the day, decided to take the new kindergarten course offered by Professor Kraus and his wife, Maria Kraus-Boelte, in New York.[14] It was through her Froebelian training with Kraus-Boelte that Marean brought the spirit of Froebel into the Ontario kindergarten. Ada Marean Hughes was later to say of Maria Kraus-Boelte:

> I believe firmly that Mrs. Kraus has given more spirituality and more reality to this great work than all the rest of us put together.
> I hope every one of her students will feel that they have a similar message to convey, and to convey it in the same spirit, and in a way that will do honour to the spirit of Froebel that lives in Mrs. Kraus and in *her* work, as I believe in *none other*, similarly employed.[15]

---

[11] Mrs. Hubbard had compiled a book of songs and games which was later used by kindergartners in Ontario. *Merry Songs and Games*, New York: Leo Fiest, 1881.

[12] Toronto, *Minutes of the Proceedings of the Public School Board*, 1882, p. 42.

[13] Toronto, *Annual Report of the Inspector of Public Schools*, 1883, pp. 25-26.

[14] Letter to the author from Laura Hughes Lunde, December 12, 1961.

[15] Pamphlet, courtesy of Mrs. Lunde, *Maria Kraus-Boelte, in Celebration of Fifty Years of Kindergarten Work - An Account of the Reception Held in New York, December 2, 1909, at the Hotel San Remo*, p. 5.

In 1885, Ada Marean married James Hughes. His first wife had died and left him with a young family to raise. Ada Marean Hughes continued to teach Froebel's theory and practices twice a week to the young women training to become kindergartners with the Toronto Board, but accepted no salary for her work, possibly because her husband felt one salary from the Toronto Board was sufficient. She continued her work until 1900.

Ada Hughes is credited with a number of accomplishments. She was founder of the Toronto Kindergarten Association. In 1892 she was a planner and charter member of the Kindergarten Section of the Ontario Educational Association and in 1900 she was elected President of the Ontario Educational Association. She was known to kindergartners throughout Ontario. It was said she never failed to give help and encouragement to those who came to discuss the kindergarten with her.

As well as linking the Ontario kindergarten to the Froebelian kindergarten, Ada Hughes also united the kindergarten in Ontario with the American kindergarten. She gave her active professional years to Ontario education but she continued her interest in the American Kindergarten Movement. She was a charter member of the International Kindergarten Union when it was founded in 1892, and was elected President of that organization in 1906, the only Canadian ever to hold that office. She also served on the Committee of Nineteen when a review of the American kindergarten was undertaken. Lorne Pierce, in speaking of her, claimed that she "became one of the best known leaders among the kindergartners of America, . . ."[16]

Once the first kindergarten class was underway, the door was opened to the Froebelian kindergarten to become part of the public school system of Ontario. The *Public School Act* of 1885 permitted boards to make provisions for children who were five years old but it was not until 1887 that the kindergarten was formally accepted in Ontario. In the *Education Act* of that year provisions were made for the organization of kindergartens and the training of teachers and, as well, a system of grants was put in place. However, the *Act* did delegate to the boards the responsibility of establishing kindergartens. The clause read as follows:

> To make regulations for the organization of schools for children between three and five years of age, to be known as kindergarten schools; to provide for the training and licensing of teachers for such schools, and to pay for their maintenance and of any appropriation made by the Legislative Assembly for Public Schools such sums of money as such kindergarten schools may be entitled to receive on a basis of average attendance.[17]

---

[16] Lorne Pierce, *Fifty Years of Public Service*, p. 94.

[17] Ontario, *Revised Statutes*, II, 1887, p. 2384 (see Frontispiece, p. viii).

In 1886, the Honourable George W. Ross, who was the Minister of Education from 1882 until 1899 when he became Premier, issued a Departmental circular urging inspectors and boards in cities, towns and villages to open kindergartens. He wrote, "I know of no way that a Board of Trustees can contribute more towards the cultivation of right methods in the elementary classes of a public school than by the establishment of a kindergarten."[18] Along with Egerton Ryerson, he envisioned the Ontario public school system as an integrated whole.

> The humblest kinder-gartener [sic] is the greatest force that comes in contact with these pupils from day to day, and she need not take second place with the president of a university. This is a profession that has no gradations. There are no jealousies in our ranks. The University takes up the work where the High School leaves it, . . . each department being *facile princeps* within its own sphere. This is the work in which we are engaged; we give intellectual life to the whole nation.[19]

The Minister received numerous inquiries about the kindergarten from boards within Ontario, other parts of Canada, the West Indies and the Orient. In Ontario most of the inquiries related to possible speakers, estimated costs of establishing kindergartens and the availability of government grants. The Department of Education frequently recommended either James Hughes or one of the kindergarten directors at the Normal Schools as a qualified speaker.

Courses for kindergarten directors were offered at the Normal Schools in both Toronto and Ottawa. The person who held the position of Director of the kindergarten at the Toronto Normal Model School also became the Inspector of Kindergartens for the province. Bessie E. Hailman from Indianapolis was the first Director in 1885.[20] Caroline M. C. Hart became Director and Inspector of Kindergartens in 1886, a position she held until 1892. She was an associate of Blow, having studied with her in St. Louis.[21] Mary

---

[18] Ontario, Department of Education, *Circular* 19 (in the Provincial Archives).

[19] *Ontario Educational Association Proceedings*, 1895, p. 65.

[20] Miss Hailman [in official records Hailman was spelled with one *n*] may have been the daughter of Dr. and Mrs. W. N. Hailmann. Dr. Hailmann translated Froebel's *Education of Man*. During the 1880's he was Superintendent of Public Schools in Laporte, Indiana. Mrs. Hailmann, in collaboration with her daughter, prepared a book of songs and games for the kindergarten. See *Pioneers of the Kindergarten in America*, prepared by the Committee of Nineteen, New York: The Century Co., 1924, p. 257.

[21] Susan Blow said of Caroline Hart, "I regard her and Miss Fisher who is now in Boston as the best trainers in America." Letter from Susan E. Blow to the Honourable George W.

E. Macintyre of Strathroy, who had received her training from Hart, was the third Director. She remained in that position until 1932. Elizabeth Bolton was appointed Kindergarten Director of the Ottawa Normal Model School Kindergarten in 1886. She continued as Director until 1917 when A. H. Baker, her former Assistant, became Director.[22]

Mary Macintyre undertook several tours of inspection throughout the province as Inspector of Kindergartens, a position she held along with her responsibilities at the Toronto Normal School. For the most part, she spoke well of the kindergartens she inspected. She did find, however, that where the teachers were not trained kindergartners the rooms were conducted like primary classes, the only difference being that kindergarten equipment and materials were used.

In 1901, Macintyre wrote to the Honourable Richard Harcourt, who had become Minister of Education, recommending that a separate appointment be made for an Inspector of Kindergartens. She felt kindergartens should be inspected twice yearly, otherwise inspectors and trustees who did not know the system were at the mercy of poor teachers.

She also felt a Provincial Kindergarten Inspector could create fresh interest in the kindergarten.[23] Several appeals to have an Inspector of Kindergartens appointed were made during subsequent years by kindergartners at the OEA as well as by Macintyre but no action was ever taken by the Department.

Toronto led the way for the establishment of kindergartens in Ontario. It was not long before other boards, recognizing its value, introduced the kindergarten into their systems. Kindergartens were opened in Hamilton in 1885, in London in 1887 and in Ottawa in 1889.

The possibility of having Kindergartens had been considered in Hamilton early in 1885. A Committee of the Board, after visiting private schools in Buffalo and discussing the kindergarten with James Hughes, recommended kindergartens be opened. A lady who had trained with Susan Blow, Fannie C. Colcord, was hired as Kindergarten Supervisor. She stayed for one year and in that time instructed four students in the kindergarten method, one of whom was Bertha Savage. W. H. Ballard, Inspector of Public Schools in Hamilton, was very pleased with the progress of the four students. "The Teachers have laboured diligently and successfully and have

---

Ross, January 15, 1887, in the Provincial Archives.

[22]Elizabeth Bolton had been a teacher in Ottawa. There was a suggestion that she had taken her kindergarten training in the United States.

---

[23]Letter from Mary Macintyre to the Honourable Richard Harcourt, November 26, 1901, in the Provincial Archives.

done all that was possible to be done in the time they have been at work. . . ."[24]

In the fall of 1886, Leontine T. Newcomb of St. Louis became Kindergarten Supervisor. By 1890 there were 14 kindergartens in Hamilton and 1,352 children enrolled.[25] Newcomb continued to supervise the work and train teachers until 1894 when Bertha Savage became head Kindergarten Director. She continued her own kindergarten class but also trained kindergarten assistants. When, in 1896, Mary Macintyre inspected the Hamilton kindergartens, she referred to Savage as "a thoroughly practical woman and an earnest worker". She thought the kindergartens would do well under her direction.[26] By 1910 there were 735 children enrolled in 16 kindergartens.[27]

In 1885, Inspector J. B. Boyle of London wrote in his report, "Our system will never be complete until we shall have a kindergarten classroom in connection with every primary school in the city."[28] John Dearness, Inspector of rural schools in Middlesex, was responsible for introducing the kindergarten into the London schools. He had discussed the idea with both Elizabeth Peabody of Boston and Leontine Newcomb of Hamilton. A kindergarten was opened in 1887 at Askin Street School in Westminster Township which was part of Dr. Dearness's Inspectorate. Within the next two years the township was annexed by the City of London.

When Caroline Hart visited London in the spring of 1892, she remarked on the enthusiasm of the Kindergartners and the keen public interest. She recommended that Agnes MacKenzie, a graduate of the Ottawa course, be made Supervisor of kindergartens. Three years later Macintyre described MacKenzie as being "ably fitted for her work both practically and theoretically".[29] She, too, was pleased with the progress of the kindergarten in London and the quality of work being done there. MacKenzie left to be married in 1905 and Jean Laidlaw, a graduate of the kindergarten course at the Toronto Normal School, became Supervisor. She promoted mothers' clubs and encouraged the Froebel Society of London to invite special lecturers.[30] She resigned in 1910 and two years

[24]Hamilton, *Minutes of the Proceedings of the Board of Education*, 1886, p. 58.

[25]*Ibid.*, 1890, p. 35.

[26]*Ibid.*, 1895, p. 45.

[27]*Ibid.*, 1910, pp. 21, 29.

[28]London, *Annual Report, the Board of Education*, 1885, p. 6.

[29]*Ibid.*, 1895, p. 32.

[30]Dr. and Mrs. Hughes were invited to speak in London. There were also speakers from other parts of Ontario and the United States. Comments were made to the author during a visit to London that this marked the beginning of University Extension work in London.

later Clara Brenton was appointed and remained Kindergarten and Primary Supervisor until her retirement in 1943.

Kindergartens were introduced into the Ottawa Public Schools in 1889. The enrolment was never high. By 1892 there were four kindergartens with a total enrolment of 167 children.[31] Georgina Lovick who had been Bolton's assistant at the Ottawa Normal School was made Director of Kindergartens. When she resigned E. J. Morris was appointed, and then in 1900 Maud Lyon was made Kindergarten Supervisor. By 1910 there were 19 kindergartens in the 20 schools, 925 children enrolled, and 41 kindergartners.[32] Comparatively few references were made to the kindergarten in Ottawa until 1910, when Dr. J H. Putman became Inspector of Public Schools.

New kindergartens were opened in Toronto each year. The Toronto Board continued to train its own teachers until the provincial system was sufficiently organized to introduce uniform examinations for Kindergarten Directors and Kindergarten Assistants.[33] By 1891 Hughes was able to say, "The desirability of making the kindergarten the foundation of a thorough educational system is no longer a debatable question."[34] By 1895 there were nearly 2,000 children attending 40 kindergartens in Toronto[35] and by 1914, 78 out of the 88 public schools had kindergartens.[36] Louise Currie, one of Ada Hughes's students, had been appointed Assistant Supervisor in 1885 and then Supervisor in 1900. She acted in that capacity until her retirement in 1925.

Kindergartens were first included in the Report of the Minister in 1892. At that time there were 66 kindergartens in the province, 6,375 children enrolled, and 160 kindergartners.[37] Kindergartens were established in the cities of Brantford, Hamilton, Kingston, London, Ottawa, St. Catharines, Stratford and Toronto; in the towns of Aylmer, Brockville, Chatham, Dundas, Ingersoll, Peterborough, Strathroy, Tillsonburg,

---

[31] Ottawa, *Minutes of the Proceedings of the Public School Board,* 1892, p. 73.

[32] *Ibid.,* 1910, pp. 9, 10. The number of kindergartners probably includes both the Directors and the assistants.

[33] By the 1890's, only certificates issued by the Department of Education were recognized as valid throughout the province.

[34] Toronto, *Annual Report. . . ,* 1891, p. 61.

[35] Toronto, *Annual Report. . . ,* 1895, pp. 16-18.

[36] Toronto, *Minutes. . . ,* 1914, Appendix, p. 1287.

[37] Ontario, *Report of the Minister. . . ,* 1892, p. xxiv.

Toronto Junction, Waterloo and Niagara Falls, and in the village of Preston.[38] By 1900 there were also kindergartens in the cities of Belleville and Guelph, the towns of Berlin (Kitchener), Galt and Owen Sound, and the villages of Ashburnham, Campbellford and Hespeler.[39] There would be no kindergartens in rural areas, however, for over forty years (*infra*, p. 88).

The kindergarten sessions, for the most part, were held during the mornings only. During these early years it was not uncommon for as many as 50 or 60 children to be enrolled in a kindergarten class. In London where classes tended to be even larger, afternoon kindergartens were soon opened. Hamilton, too, introduced an afternoon session. The children in the kindergarten classes were guided by a director and usually one assistant. Unpaid students in training also assisted the director.

There was a great deal of enthusiasm surrounding the kindergarten during the first two decades of its history in Ontario. In part, it was the enthusiasm of educators caught up in the New Education Movement. Kindergartens were opened in cities, towns and villages throughout Ontario. Requests came to the Department of Education from many inside and outside the province seeking information about their establishment.

Kindergarten associations were organized, including in 1892, the Kindergarten Section of the OEA. The Kindergarten courses offered at the Normal Schools in Ottawa and Toronto attracted many young women into the profession. Enthusiasm was also heightened by frequent contacts with the American Kindergarten Movement.

The kindergarten continued to expand in most centres where it had been established. However, as the initial enthusiasm began to wane, the young kindergarten was faced with not a few difficulties. Some of the smaller towns even discontinued their classes. Unfortunately, the idea of the kindergarten was not always understood and certainly there were private citizens as well as educators who thought it an expensive fad. Agnes MacKenzie of London expressed her concern about the criticisms in these words:

> It is regarded in the light of a new kind of play, for the conduct of which little or no training is required – or of a nursery where babies are taken in charge – in order that their mothers may have more leisure for running about. The very last thing to be appreciated is the educational value.[40]

Another difficulty was the tendency on the part of many to think of

---

[38]*Ibid.*, 1892, p. 60.

[39]*Ibid.*, 1900, p. 72.

[40]Agnes E. MacKenzie, "Kindergarten Extension," *Ontario Educational Association...*, 1894, p. 176.

the kindergarten as something quite apart from the school. J. H. Putman of Ottawa clarified this point of view in a statement in which he showed his agreement with the kindergarten pedagogy but not its organization:

> The [kindergartners] have allowed it to be assumed that the kindergarten was one thing and the rest of the school something quite different. . . . They have even assumed that the kindergarten teacher needs a special psychology. They have encouraged the public to believe that kindergarten philosophy, method, and practices are so profound that they can be mastered only by a select few among well-educated people and after years of study. All this has tended to foster the idea that the kindergarten was a fine thing to have but that it was really something different from an ordinary school and, therefore, something which might be done without.[41]

Kindergartners were very concerned that the kindergarten was being misunderstood. They had a missionary zeal in attempting to make the kindergarten and its educational purposes clear. The members of the Kindergarten Section of the OEA continually urged the spread of both kindergartens and Froebelian ideas. The local Froebel Societies were encouraged to suggest speakers and offer assistance in centres where there was no kindergarten or where there was no association to support the kindergartner. Leontine Newcomb of Hamilton expressed the unity of purpose that kindergartners needed in order to make the kindergarten better known:

> No one can be sufficient unto himself nor is any one person's single experience of much avail, for we become strong as we work in harmony with others, and give and take from the general fund of experience.[42]

However, it was difficult for the kindergartners themselves to coordinate plans for the advancement of the kindergarten throughout the province.

Even in Toronto where the kindergarten had been accepted and had experienced its most rapid growth, there were difficulties. In 1893 James Hughes reiterated the value of the kindergarten to the Toronto Board when the educational idea again came under attack. To him, the kindergarten was the foundation of a democratic public school system; acting as a bridge it harmonized the home with the school. Furthermore, the kindergarten provided for the child's all-sided development - physically, mentally and spiritually.[43]

---

[41]Ottawa, *Minutes. . .* , 1913, p. 43.

[42]*Ontario Educational Association. . .* , 1892, pp. 33, 34

[43]Toronto, *Annual Report. . .* , 1893, pp. 19-30.

James L. Hughes (1846-1935) was a visionary who recognized the worth of the Froebelian Kindergarten and gave it his full support. He was the only Canadian to write extensively about Froebel's plans for education. In his book, *Froebel's Educational Laws,* which was published in 1899,[44] he acknowledged his indebtedness to his wife, Ada Marean Hughes, for her inspiration and helpful suggestions.

James Hughes was also well known to American educators. He had addressed the American Superintendents' Association at different times on various aspects of kindergarten education. He was the first President of the New York State Kindergarten Association. He was also a personal friend of several American educators. Lorne Pierce claimed that James Hughes "lectured on different phases of the Froebelian philosophy in 132 towns and cities of the United States and in some 200 towns and cities of the British Isles and Canada".[45]

Certainly, as Chief Inspector of Public Schools in Toronto, Hughes had a dynamic impact on public education. He was credited with introducing manual training and domestic science, cadets and the penny bank into the schools. He approved of attractive classrooms and home gardening. He opposed the use of corporal punishment and worked to abolish a system of promotions based solely on examinations. Furthermore, he promoted the Froebelian kindergarten. In his thesis, "Changing Conceptions of Discipline and Pupil-Teacher Relations in Canadian Schools", F. H. Johnson, in summarizing the educational contributions of Dr. Hughes, claimed that Hughes was the "leading exponent of Froebelianism in Canada".

Largely through the abundant energy of Hughes these Froebelian views were well publicized in Canada, both in the educational journals to which he was a frequent contributor and in the eight books on education which he wrote. He was probably our most prolific writer in the field of education, the leading exponent of the Kindergarten and of Froebelian philosophy, and one of the most influential minds in Canadian education.[46]

Men and women such as James Hughes and his wife, as well as the leading kindergartners in the other cities and those involved in teacher training in the Normal Schools, tried to present the Froebelian kindergarten both forcefully and clearly. Nonetheless, as is so often the case, the visionaries outdistanced common practice. Some kindergartners, too, were thwarted

---

[44]James L. Hughes, *Froebel's Educational Laws*, New York; D. Appleton & Co., 1899.

[45]Pierce, *Fifty Years of Public Service*, p. 7.

[46]F. H. Johnson, *Changing Conceptions of Discipline and Pupil-Teacher Relations in Canadian Schools* (unpublished doctoral dissertation, University of Toronto, 1952), p. 199.

from utilizing Froebel's principles fully because of the large enrolment in a kindergarten class. Then, too, there were those who lacked insight into Froebel's system and tried to "teach" in the sense of "instruct" the kindergarten children. As a result, one could find kindergartens in Ontario which reflected varying degrees of Froebelianism.

Summary

By the 1870's, largely through the efforts of Dr. Ryerson, the school system of Ontario was ready to be extended and to diversify. The first kindergarten was opened in Toronto in 1883. Kindergartens received official recognition from the Department of Education in 1885 and two years later were allotted a share in the provincial grant. A training course was introduced into the Normal Schools, first in Toronto and then in Ottawa. Kindergartens were opened in Hamilton in 1885, London in 1887 and Ottawa in 1889. By 1900 there were kindergartens in 10 cities, 14 towns and four villages.

The leaders of the Kindergarten Movement in Ontario were followers of Froebel. Ada Marean Hughes had received her kindergarten training from Maria Kraus-Boelte who had been a pupil of Froebel's widow, thus linking the kindergarten in Ontario with the true Froebelian spirit. James Hughes of Toronto was an ardent supporter of the Froebelian kindergarten. Other educators supported Froebelian theories and practices; Elizabeth Bolton and Georgina Lovick of Ottawa, Leontine Newcomb and Bertha Savage of Hamilton, Agnes MacKenzie and Jean Laidlaw of London and in Toronto Caroline Hart, Mary Macintyre and Louise Currie. Froebel Societies were founded in the various cities and by 1892 the Kindergarten Section of the Ontario Educational Association was formed.

The kindergarten was buoyed up on a wave of enthusiasm during the first two decades of its history. Then, it began to meet with difficulties. Certainly there were those who failed to recognize the educational value of the kindergarten. Some considered it to be an expensive fad, while others claimed its only purpose was to free mothers from the responsibility of childrearing. Still others thought of it as a cult quite separate from the rest of the school. However, there were kindergartners who tried to present the true ideas of the Froebelian kindergarten in Ontario, although it was difficult for them to co-ordinate their efforts, especially when the Department of Education failed to appoint a Provincial Inspector of Kindergartens. The views of these kindergartners and other supporters of the Kindergarten Movement are important as we continue to look at the development of Froebel's Kindergarten in Ontario.

CHAPTER IV

THE EDUCATIONAL THEORIES AND PRACTICES OF THE EARLY KINDERGARTEN

The Froebelian Doctrine of Unity

The Froebelian doctrine of unity, that the harmony of life was found in God and thus there was a harmony between God, humankind and nature, was accepted by Ontario educators. James Hughes, the outstanding spokesman for the Froebelian cause, claimed that the harmony found in God was the "co-ordinating element in all life-processes".[1] Leontine Newcomb of Hamilton referred, too, to the harmony inherent in God's love. Both agreed with Froebel that the business of the school was to reveal to the child the harmony in all of life. Hughes would lead the child "to see God as love, life, and the centre of all unifying and uplifting powers".[2]

There was also agreement that nature had a significant influence upon child development. To Froebel and to the early kindergartners, nature was like a book which revealed God's beauty as well as His laws. Ada Marean Hughes, in an article in the *Canada School Journal*, expressed her understanding of the meaning which nature could have for the child:

His ears are open to the varied music of nature. In everything he finds pleasure, because of his intimate acquaintance with and sympathy for everything that God has made.[3]

The harmonious relationship of the child with others, which began within the circle of the family, was extremely significant in child development. James Hughes referred to the good effect family life could have upon the child. To him, the beginnings of both religious life and community life were fostered in the family. Ada Hughes stressed the importance of bringing the home and the school into harmony with each other. She encouraged mothers' meetings where mothers and kindergartners could become more closely of one mind in promoting child development.

Froebel's central aim in education was to bring each child to God so that the child might be developed harmoniously from within himself in all his relationships to humankind and nature. Hughes could only agree with Froebel's aim. The well-loved child would develop both harmoniously and fully.

While many educators accepted Froebel's aim, there were some who

---

[1] James L. Hughes, *Froebel's Educational Laws* (New York: D. Appleton & Co., 1899), p. 48.

[2] *Ibid.*, p. 279.

[3] Ada Maren [*sic*.], "The Kindergarten as Related to the Nursery and School," *Canada School Journal*, II (March 1878), p. 53.

began to place an equal emphasis upon other objectives. In 1896, W. H. Ballard of Hamilton referred to the kindergarten as the best preparation for primary work. Agnes MacKenzie of London stressed the Froebelian view of the importance of kindergarten and home relationships. Ada Hughes supported Froebel's plan for the kindergarten, that it truly be "the bridge from the nursery to the school".[4]

Child development became another important aim of kindergartners. They urged the development of the whole child - his physical, mental and spiritual development. A. H. Baker of Ottawa did remind them, however, that they should not proceed "as though the full rounding of the physical, mental, and moral life were to be completed in the kindergarten".[5]

Views of Child Development and the Curriculum

There was no doubt that the enthusiasts of the new education placed the emphasis upon child development rather than upon the curriculum. They heartily believed the curriculum should serve to develop the child. Thus, they emphasized the child's self-activity and creativity over the repetition of facts, passive listening and imitation.

The early kindergartners accepted the Froebelian view that a child who was nurtured in the love of God developed from within. They referred to this inner development as "growth". Dr. Hughes believed that a child who developed in harmony with God, humankind and nature developed at peace from within himself. Ada Hughes wrote, "It [the child] does not need to be taught before it begins to grow – it has within itself the means of development,..."[6] Leontine Newcomb referred to the "continued logical development of the three-fold powers of the child in the work of head, hand, and heart".[7] *Growth* became a watchword of the early kindergarten.

Educators became aware of a need to study the child. In 1901, Ada Hughes was on the forefront of educational thinking when she declared to the kindergartners at the OEA, "We are shaking off tradition's shackles and have begun to study the individual child and suit his training to his needs."[8] How contemporary such a comment sounds to us! Later James Hughes was to write, "The real advances in child training are made by those who study the child to discover his individual powers and to reveal them gradually to

---

[4] *Ibid.*, p. 51.

[5] *Ontario Educational Association Proceedings* (1910), p. 235.

[6] Maren [*sic.*], p. 52.

[7] Hamilton, *Minutes of the Proceedings of the Board of Education* (1889), p. 56.

[8] *Ontario Educational Association. . .* (1901), p. 84.

him, . . ."[9]   Mary Macintyre emphasized method along with child study. In 1913 when she spoke to the kindergartners at the OEA she claimed, "Only a constant study of our children, and a parallel study of our methods will enable us to get the results." [10]

Toward the end of the nineteenth century Charles Darwin's theory of evolution began to influence the interpretation given Froebel's statements concerning child development. The theory of evolution converged with the thinking of the German idealistic philosophers. As a result, there was a growing feeling of optimism that by the evolutionary process mankind and the world would become better and better. The theory of evolution, as it applied to education, suggested that a carefully selected educational program could produce better persons. In German idealistic philosophy there was the thought that by reason a person could attain to the Divine or to God. Educators seemed to combine these ideas and felt that if a child, by reason and insight, grew towards God, the world could become a better place. And in this they saw progress.

Where these thoughts differed from a Froebelian view was in making growth *toward* God the aim. To Froebel, God was not only the goal, but he was also Creator and Sustainer of all things. Froebel claimed that a child who was *first* brought to God and nurtured in his love would be developed harmoniously from within. At the time, however, educators tended to interpret the child's relationship to God as a lifelong search rather than, as Froebel intended, the foundation of his development. Whichever the interpretation, Hughes wrote, "Evolution is now one of the central ideas of education. We owe it largely to Froebel."[11]

The large number of children in Ontario kindergartens (there could be anywhere from 50 to 100 children in a class[12]), limited both the children's and the kindergartner's activities. Kindergartners found they could utilize Froebel's general laws of child development but that they could not give an individual child either the freedom or the attention he required. Early in the 1900's, A. V. Aylesworth of Chatham, in an address to the kindergarten Section of the OEA, complained that kindergartners did not have sufficient time to talk with a child owing to the large kindergarten enrolment.

The idea that the kindergarten should be the foundation of the public school system was accepted by Ontario educators. George Ross claimed that

---

[9] James L. Hughes, *Training the Children* (New York; A. S. Barnes Co., 1917), p. 148.

[10] *Ontario Education Association. . .* (1913), p. 238.

[11] James L. Hughes, *Froebel's . . ,* p. 264.

[12] John Millar, *The Educational System of the Province of Ontario* (Toronto: Warwick & Sons, 1893), p. 12.

the kindergarten was the basis of all sound primary instruction. James Hughes referred to it as an essential part of any democratic school system. "The kindergarten should not be an appendage to the Public School system, for a favoured part of the school population. It should be a part of the school system, its foundation, . . ."[13] Leontine Newcomb, who was supported in her view by Inspector Ballard, claimed that the Froebelian kindergarten was the only possible foundation for a public school system in which each child was to be developed into a responsible citizen.

> By the influence of the schools a nation has power to determine her own destiny. True citizenship as well as intellectual development is the keystone to the "national arch", and public education must cement the structure.
> This foundation must be laid with the youngest as well as the oldest child in our Schools; and the Froebelian Kindergarten, while completely adapted to the first three or four years of the child's schooling, must reach out through all the later periods of his education, as the fundamental principle of all life growth and development.[14]

The kindergarten curriculum in the early days was Froebelian. It included Christianity, physical health, sense training, Froebel's games and finger plays, nature study, language and literature, mathematics, music, art (the Occupations) and play with the Froebel Gifts. At the beginning of the half-day session the children, marching to music, brought their chairs to the circle and sat down for the opening exercises, which consisted of a hymn, a prayer, songs and discussion. Two separate half-hour periods were usually set aside for play with the Gifts and a complementary Art Occupation. When the children played with the Gifts, a small group sat on either side of a table, the top of which was marked in inch squares, and the kindergartner sat at one end.

Mary Macintyre was concerned that all the activities which were included in the kindergarten program would actually further child development. "All work, to be successful, must be logically and definitely carried out from week to week, not with rigid adherence to a program book, but with clear insight into the necessities and experiences of the children."[15] She opposed the introduction of any academic work such as printing and reading into the Froebelian kindergarten program; instead, she believed it was important that the educational foundations be laid through the child's play.

[13] Toronto, *Annual Report of the Inspector of Public Schools* (1893), p. 23.

[14] Hamilton, *Minutes*. . . (1889), p. 50.

[15] Ontario, *Report of the Minister of Education* (1896), p. 232.

During the early years there was no course of study for the kindergarten and there were very few program books available. In some centres the Kindergarten Supervisor met with the kindergartners each week and outlined the program to them. Generally, she planned the week's program around a theme. Thus, it became common practice to develop the program from themes, using the seasons or special events.

Emotional Development

Educators agreed with Froebel that the child grew from within outwardly; thus it was important that his heart and sympathies be nurtured. Hughes wrote, "The inner must be the centre from which the life power springs."[16] Froebel had written for mothers as well as kindergartners and kindergartners agreed that the home had the primary responsibility for the child's emotional development. They could never replace the home, particularly the mother's influence, but they could provide an accepting atmosphere.

Spiritual Development

The atmosphere in the kindergarten was to be a loving one. Educators agreed the child came to know God from the love shared in the family, through nature and by Christian teaching. Hughes believed the child

should be taught the Christian religion but he felt dogmas must never be forced upon a child. That a youngster experience Christian love was what was most important. Georgina Lovick of Ottawa brought to the attention of the kindergartners at the OEA the importance of guiding the child in a loving manner in reflection of God's love. Further, the kindergartners agreed with Froebel that it was as a child used his powers for good that he grew in an understanding of God.

Social Development

While the home provided the child with his first social experience, the kindergarten could offer a wider social environment. Ways of helping a child develop socially were suggested to kindergartners. Leontine Newcomb believed the child should be encouraged to act "in harmony with others as a matter of choice".[17] Ada Hughes felt social development involved experiences of learning to give as well as to receive. James Hughes, recognizing Christianity to be basic to social development, suggested that it was in knowing God as Heavenly Father and, therefore, all men as brothers, that the child would become aware of his social responsibility.

Social studies was not a term used by early kindergartners, but the children were taken on excursions into the community, played games in imitation of the adult's world of work

---

[16]James L. Hughes, *Froebel's . . .* , p. 244.

[17]Hamilton, *Minutes. . .* (1889), p. 54.

and listened to stories about their world. Festival days, including a Christmas closing and a spring festival, were celebrated in the kindergarten and parents were usually invited.

Physical Development

Educators in Ontario acknowledged the importance of the child's physical health and activity in his education. James Hughes commented on the relationship of the child's physical health to his mental activity and thus to the development of his character. He approved of the way in which Froebel's Gifts aided the development of the child's neurological system, particularly the coordination of the mind and hand. After the Boer War (1899-1902), a time when Britons came to realize the importance of good physical health, more attention was paid to the physical well-being of children in Ontario schools.[18] Kindergartners were also concerned that the child be given the freedom to express his inner development through physical activity.

Kindergartners were familiar with Susan Blow's translation of Froebel's *Mother Play*.[19] They recognized that they, too, had the responsibility of complementing the mother's efforts in nurturing the child. While they agreed that the mother had the initial responsibility of developing the child's five senses, kindergartners used Froebel's games and plays to stimulate the child's senses of sight, hearing, touch, taste and smell. Bolton reminded them that the senses were the doors to the inner child and, therefore, needed definite training.[20]

Games

Ontario kindergartners accepted Froebel's games as ones which would develop the inner child as well as provide him with suitable physical activity for the development of skills. Jean Laidlaw of London, in speaking to the kindergartners at the OEA, revealed a great deal of insight into Froebel's games.

> The games employ the *whole* child, body as well as mind, and it is especially important in considering them to remind ourselves of the effect of our actions in determining the child's spiritual life.[21]

She went on to say, "The more joy in the spirit of the games, the more power have they to develop the children."[22]

---

[18]Medical and dental inspections were introduced into Ontario schools during the first decade of the twentieth century.

[19]Froebel's *Mother Play* was on the required reading list of the Kindergarten course offered at the Normal Schools.

[20]*Ontario Educational Association. . .* (1892), p. 128.

[21]Jean R. Laidlaw, "The Spirit and Method of the Games," *Ontario Educational Association. . .* , pp. 180, 181.

[22]*Ibid.*, p. 275.

Mary Macintyre, too, emphasized the importance of the spirit in which the games were played.

Nature

In Froebel's educational plan nature walks helped the child understand the world in which he lived while the care of pets and plants helped him to discover God's laws. As well, in the care of living things he learned to accept responsibility. James Hughes supported Froebel's views. "His [the child's] garden work teaches him that the growth of plants does not depend upon himself or upon human power, but that an invisible power governs it."[23] To Hughes, caring for gardens and pets helped the child learn to work in partnership with God, while nature walks developed in him an appreciation for God's world.

Nature walks, gardening and the care of pets could not always be arranged for kindergarten children in city schools but these children could walk to a park, if one were close by. Most kindergartens had windowboxes and indoor plants, although a few had gardens. Some kindergartens had canaries or rabbits for pets. Macintyre was impressed by the provisions for nature study in the London kindergartens. "The kindergartens are sunny, pretty, home-like rooms, with plants under the care of the children,

and animals which they feed and protect."[24]

Language Development

Ontario educators agreed with Froebel that language involved the child in life. It was through language that the child came to understand his experiences and, further, that he was able to express himself. Experiences were the basis of the child's language development. To James Hughes, experience led to accurate thinking and this in turn resulted in accurate expression. He wrote, "Clear, strong thoughts never lack expression."[25]

Kindergartners read and told many stories to the children – nature stories, animal stories, Bible stories, stories of everyday events, fairytales and legends. Macintyre encouraged kindergartners to tell stories where good and evil were truly distinguishable. However, with the large numbers of children in a kindergarten, few kindergartners seemed to have sufficient time to listen to every child relate his experiences and then, as Froebel had suggested, weave them into a story.

It was necessary for each child to have opportunities for personal expression. Newcomb urged kindergartners to give the child ample

---

[23]James L. Hughes, *Froebel's. . .* , pp. 180, 181.

[24]Ontario, *Report of the Minister. . .* (1896), p. 231.

[25]James L. Hughes, *Froebel's. . .* , p.241.

opportunity to express his own thoughts. Plays and dramatizations were also considered useful ways to develop the child's oral language expression.

Reading was not considered a suitable activity for four and five-year-old children in the kindergarten. Richard Harcourt, Minister of Education, in expressing his views of early reading, referred to a report by W. T. Harris who at that time was Federal Commissioner of Education in the United States. Dr. Harris supported the stand of no reading in the kindergarten.

The child does not learn to read in the true kindergarten. It is too abrupt a transition from the home to require the child to learn a new language, the language addressed to the eye instead of a language addressed to the ear, and to become eye-minded instead of ear-minded at the age of four or five years.[26]

Intellectual Development

Educators agreed with Froebel that the child formed impressions of the world through his own experiences. Ada Hughes claimed concrete experiences gave the child opportunities to form impressions. It was upon such impressions that abstract learning would later be built.

Ideas must first be received from intimate knowledge of *real* things before the abstract work of the school is begun; as soon as the mind demands *much* food, it should be supplied, but in limited quantities at first. Though a child trained in a kindergarten, from the age of three or [to] seven years, does not call words at sight, or tell, with parrot-like precision, the letters which compose those words, his mind has been filled with facts and ideas worth infinitely more to him than any mechanical memorizing could possibly be. He has acquired a practical knowledge of the elementary principles of number, and can apply those principles intelligently, without knowing whether the process by which he is to determine his results is known as addition, subtraction, multiplication, or division.[27]

Ontario kindergartners believed the manufactured Gifts and Occupations provided the child with suitable concrete experiences. They thought the sequential development of the Gifts would enable a child to discover relationships. The child was to begin with the simple and the known and then progress towards the complex and the unknown. However, in order to give the child a harmonious experience, there was always a return to the familiar, the simple and the known.

---

[26]Ontario, *Report of the Minister. . .* (1903), pp. xv-xvi.

[27]Ada Maren [*sic*.], *op. cit.*, p. 53.

Newcomb stated, "The more learning is reduced to the simplest principles, and the more thoroughly we teach them, the more will be learned."[28]

James Hughes discussed the importance of problem solving in a child's intellectual development. He wanted the problems to be ones the child met with in his play. He ranked problem finding equally with problem solving.

> The first eight years should be devoted in the homes and in the schools to the solving of the problems which the children find themselves, first by making their own plans, and then by achieving their plans for transforming the materials that are most interesting to them.[29]

Mathematics

Kindergartners were enthusiastic about the mathematical concepts behind the Gifts and Occupations. They believed that a child in his play with the Gifts and Occupations, if he were guided by the kindergartner, would come to an understanding of form, size and number. Furthermore, he would become familiar with geometrical shapes and form ideas of space and time. Ada Hughes believed the fourth

Gift, which consisted of eight brick-shaped blocks, was especially useful in developing mathematical impressions within the child.

To James Hughes as to Froebel, mathematics was a dynamic study. Hughes claimed mathematics did not lead to the discovery of space relationships but rather resulted from them.[30] He was very much opposed to instructing a child in the use of the Gifts. Instead he would allow the child in his play to form impressions of mathematical ideas.

Music and Art

The songs and singing games were recognized as one of the most attractive features of the Froebelian kindergarten. Folk traditions were preserved and at the same time the songs were a means of self-expression for the child. Educators agreed with Froebel that the words of the songs and games were yet another way of helping the child to understand his world. They also believed that music had a spiritual significance in that it reached into the child's heart and spirit.

Rhythmical movement was included in the program, although it took the form of children marching around the room in time with the musical accompaniment. Possibly the large classes made it difficult for kindergartners to allow children the freedom they needed to interpret the

---

[28]Hamilton, *Minutes.* . . (1889), p. 55.

[29]James L. Hughes, *Training the Children,* p. 48.

[30]James L. Hughes, *Froebel's.* . . , p. 82.

rhythm for themselves. Jean Laidlaw gave the older children freedom for rhythmic interpretation but she felt the younger children needed guidance.[31] Pianos were used in the kindergartens to accompany the singing and the rhythms. As well, simple tunes and chords played on the piano indicated the next activity to the children.

Art was developed through the Occupations. Froebel had stressed forms of beauty, forms of knowledge and forms of life. The child learned the laws of symmetry and design from the Froebelian forms of beauty. Forms of life should have been free drawings but very often the child drew the object on a paper lined in half-inch squares. Kindergartners agreed that a child needed to observe an object carefully before attempting to draw it, however. Thus, drawing, too, helped a child to understand his world. Both crayons and paints were used in the early kindergartens. Once the child completed his piece of art it was pasted into an Occupations scrapbook.

By the 1900's, however, the Froebelian Occupations came under attack. There were criticisms against the fine handwork and the design patterns, as well as the advanced forms required from a child. In 1899, J. W. Milne of Odessa, in a speech delivered at the OEA to the kindergartners, severely censured the way Froebel's Art Occupations were being used.

Lines as lines, angles, circles, etc., are foreign to the child; he sees them nowhere in nature, and they possess no interest for him. Sequences in paper-folding and piecework are sequences too advanced for him. He gets good from handling the material but not from making complex forms or weaving intricate designs.[32]

Although such criticisms made educators in Ontario question the value of the art occupations, they continued to be used in a complementary way to the Gifts for many years. Some of the activities required by kindergartners were small and intricate for little hands to accomplish. However, larger materials were gradually introduced.

Creativity

Ontario kindergartners accepted the Froebelian view that each person was creative because he was created in the image of God. Thus each child should be encouraged to express himself in creative self-activity. A. V. Aylesworth of Chatham revealed her understanding of Froebel's view when she referred to the child's creative self-activity as divine energy. Ada Hughes also believed that the child's creativity was best expressed when the child, acting in partnership with God, exerted himself to the limits of his energy.

---

[31]*Ontario Educational Association...* (1906), p. 56.

[32]J. W. Milne, "The Relation of Art to the Other Studies in Education," *Ontario Educational Association...* (1899), p. 326.

The man who would live near the Divine is not the one who sits in passive contemplation of what has been, but the one who works to the uttermost limit of his power that he may feel the joy of living contact with divine life in cooperative creation.[33]

With Froebel, she emphasized the benefits to the child gained through his effort and striving even though the creative product appeared to be insignificant.

James Hughes referred to two stages of creativity. In the beginning, the child learned to use materials in ways which were original to him. Hughes felt the kindergarten Occupations provided the child with suitable types of materials for creative art expression.

There the children are working with real things, developing their creative powers by planning things and achieving them under the direction of simple fundamental laws, getting all their mental development by making things and transforming conditions logically. Their achieving power is developed as the chief centre of power and character.[34]

Then, once the child, maturing into an adult, had mastered the known, he was ready to make an original contribution to the accumulated wisdom of mankind.

The early kindergartners found it difficult to foster creativity within the child. When Macintyre inspected kindergartens during the 1890's she found little attention was paid to the development of a child's creative power. She referred to the songs and games as well as to the ways in which the Gifts and Occupations were used. The difficulty which kindergartners had, however, in fostering the child's creativity may have been partly due to the large numbers of children in the kindergarten and thus to the lack of time the kindergartner had to listen to and guide individual children.

Educational Methods

The kindergarten was introduced into a school system where the common practice was for the teacher to instruct and the children to listen, in order that they might learn principal facts and ideas.[35] Froebel advocated a method which was the reverse of tradition, a method in which the child was self-active while much of the educator's time was spent in listening to the child and in observing him. From such study the kindergartner could plan how to further his education and development.

---

[33]*Ontario Educational Association. . .* (1901), p. 77.

[34]James L. Hughes, *Training the Children*, p. 79.

[35]When Pestalozzi's object lessons were introduced into the schools many teachers instructed the children, discussing with them the characteristics of the object, but very seldom gave each child an object to hold.

Froebel's method was, therefore, not easily understood. Educators tended to refer to the kindergarten as a "kindergarten school" where children were "instructed" by means of "amusing plays" and "toys" called the Gifts and Occupations. It was difficult for them to put into practice Froebel's intent that children should be *developed*, not "schooled" or "instructed"; the idea expressed in the word, *kindergarten*, which was a garden of children. James Hughes and his wife believed the child grew from within as he expressed himself in creative ways and self-activity. During his early years that activity was play. Therefore, they supported Froebel's method, that the kindergartner was to guide the child's play.

The atmosphere in the kindergarten needed to be one in which the child had freedom but at the same time one in which he was loved and protected. Kindergartners were in agreement, at least in theory, that a child could only attain inner freedom through self-activity.[36] But they were puzzled as to how they could give the child the freedom he needed and yet maintain order, especially if they had 50 or more children in the room. Hughes claimed a child needed freedom to plan and to execute his own plan in his own way. Macintyre, as Inspector of Kindergartens, urged that a proper balance be maintained between order

and freedom so that freedom would not become licence.

Play [37]

Play is not restricted to any one exercise or to any one hour in the kindergarten. Its spirit underlies the exercises with gifts and occupations as well as the circle games,

This opinion was expressed by Jean Laidlaw of London to the kindergartners at the OEA.[38] The spirit of play was the spirit of the Froebelian kindergarten. It was not a frivolous spirit, for the kindergartners likened the spirit of the child's play to the joy an adult experienced in his work. Mary Macintyre felt the kindergarten in Ontario needed more of that play spirit. She was aware that in some kindergartens the activities were performed in a perfunctory manner.

The idea of play being the method of education used in kindergartens met with critical opposition. Agnes MacKenzie of London spoke of the difficulties in having educators and parents understand the play method. Macintyre, too, was aware that many found it difficult to accept play as the first method of education, especially when combined with the thought that

---

[36]Georgine Lovick, "The Importance of Kindergarten Training to the Youth of Canada," *Ontario Educational Association. . .* (1896), pp. 396-99. See also Hughes, *Froebel's Educational Laws*, p. 100.

[37]For Froebel's definition of play see Chapter II, pp. 32-3.

[38]Jean Laidlaw, *op. cit.*, p. 273.

the kindergarten should be the foundation of the educational system. Opponents wanted that foundation to be work! By 1913, Macintyre admitted that the Froebelian method of play had met with defeat. It was neither understood nor accepted by educators in Ontario. With a keen sense of failure, she felt herself as well as the Kindergarten Movement responsible for not being able to convey the right interpretation of play. Furthermore, she realized that Maria Montessori's ideas were receiving a great deal of attention because it was claimed that the young children in the *Casa dei Bambini* learned to work.[39]

The Froebelian method of education which was guidance of a child's play was further eroded by the idea of free play. As early as 1896 Macintyre warned kindergartners that they would have to guard against "indefinite, capricious plays".[40] Laidlaw claimed that a child left to himself in play became "aimless" or "frivolous".[41] Nevertheless, the American Free Play Movement eventually did have an influence upon the kindergarten in Ontario and before the middle of the twentieth century free play did become a part of the kindergarten program (*infra*, pp. 78-81.)

---

[39]*Ontario Educational Association. . .* (1913), p. 236.

[40]Ontario, *Report of the Minister. . .* (1986), p. 232.

[41]Laidlaw, *op. cit.*, p. 275.

Guidance and Direction

James and Ada Hughes agreed with Froebel's suggestion that the kindergartner should be a guide. The kindergartner was to follow the child's course of development, protect him from harmful influences and provide him with whatever was necessary for his full development. The kindergartners' suggestions needed to be appropriate and timely for each child but never offered in such a way that the play would be interrupted or interfered with.

> There is no *hurry*, and no *cramming* done. The kindergartner, if she has the true spirit, gives no assistance until the little one has reached the extent of its own ability, and when suggesting or assisting, allows the child to proceed alone as soon as a fresh idea has been presented, or a new line of thought has opened the way for independent action.[42]

There was agreement that neither parents nor kindergartners should weaken the child by doing for him what he could do for himself.

Both Ada and James Hughes, in support of the Froebelian method of play, emphasized the guidance aspects of the kindergartner's role. The child was to be free in his play so that he would form impressions of his world and he learned, in the first instance,

---

[42]Ada Maren [*sic*.], *op. cit.*, p. 52.

through his own experience. The kindergartner was responsible for providing or arranging for the appropriate experience. Then she was to guide the child in a logical way through the experience by means of language and song, so that he would form clear and accurate impressions and discover relationships. They did agree that Froebel's plays, especially those with the Gifts and Occupations, provided the child with very suitable experiences.

A child also needed guidance to prevent him from behaving badly. Ada Hughes advocated that kindergartners guide the child in such a way that bad traits would not grow within him. James Hughes wanted the child to be made aware that he, too, along with all of nature, was subject to God's laws. Those laws were to be cultivated within each child so that they would become the basis for the child's self-control. Such inner self-discipline was life-giving, not restrictive.

James Hughes agreed with Froebel that each person was created in the image of God. However, he was aware that man did not always live up to the good purposes for which God had created him. Hughes believed sin had marred the child's development, although he did not believe that a child was totally depraved. To him, each child was a child of God. "But the image of the Divine is still in each of them, and it will respond to considerate sympathy, and just treatment, and opportunities to take its rightful part in the play and in the work of its new life

on terms of true recognition, and fair partnership."[43]

Not all educators had the same understanding of Froebel's educational method as did Ada and James Hughes. Certainly directed types of lessons were used in the early kindergarten, particularly with the toys, the Froebel Gifts, and their complementary Art Occupations. In these "lessons" the kindergartner "told" the group of children what to do. Such kindergarten "teachers", in their desire to make the child aware of the possibilities in the activity, also told the children how and where they were to place the blocks and the art materials. The sequential development of the Gifts was emphasized exactly. Rules and routines of the play were also taught by means of directed lessons.

Two very different approaches, then, guidance and direction, were used by kindergartners in the early kindergarten in Ontario. The former was the true Froebelian method, the guidance of a child's play. The child was free to play but protected from harm or danger and guided by the kindergartner's interaction and timely suggestions. In directed lessons, the second method, the child's activity was closely prescribed, although the child might be given some time for free play at the end of the lesson.

---

[43]James L.Hughes, *Training the Children*, p. 111

Equipment and Materials

The Froebelian Gifts and Occupations were used in the early kindergartens. The Gifts, unlike Froebel's own, were made of wood rather than soft, pliable materials. Their shapes could not be changed the way Froebel's toys had been to demonstrate the relationships between solids, surfaces, lines and points. The cubes of the Gifts were wooden blocks of one inch while the bricks were two inches in length and a half-inch thick. The seventh, eighth, ninth and tenth Gifts were the tablets, sticks, rings and lentils.

Ontario educators accepted the Gifts and Occupations as symbolic of fundamental forms in nature. The child, through play with the Gifts, acquired impressions of his world. The Art Occupations complemented the Gifts in that they provided the child with materials suitable for his creative expression. Hughes believed the Froebelian Gifts and Occupations did stimulate the child's activity.

Educators felt the child's total development – physical, intellectual and spiritual – was furthered through playing with the Gifts and Occupations because the child was actively involved. In the Ontario Department of Education *Syllabus of Studies and Regulations for Kindergartens*, printed in 1908, a statement referring to child development through the correct use of the Gifts and Occupations was included. "Through the Material, the intellectual powers are nourished, the senses are trained, interest is stimulated, constructive imagination is cultivated, and a basis is laid for the formation of good intellectual, moral and physical habits."[44]

Kindergartners, in keeping with the Froebelian tradition, encouraged the child, especially at Christmas time, to make presents for the members of his family from the materials of the Occupations. Such activity required a combination of heart, head and hand. Leontine Newcomb of Hamilton felt consideration shown for others contributed towards the child's moral development while Ada Hughes believed the child's striving in making a present for someone he loved did much to further his all-round development.

The Froebelian routine in playing with the Gifts was followed. The child placed the Gift box upside down on the table. He carefully drew out the lid and lifted the box from the blocks. Thus, he saw at the beginning of the play the blocks of the Gift as one unit and could begin to make plans for how he was going to use them. The child then placed the box with its lid under his chair.

Other equipment used in the early kindergartens included beads and the laces to string them, slats, tile boards and pegs, plasticine and sand tables.

[44]Ontario, Department of Education, *Syllabus of Studies and Regulations for Kindergartens, 1908* (Toronto: L. K. Cameron, 1908), p. 1.

Summary: A Comparison of the Early Kindergarten in Ontario with Froebel's Kindergarten

One significant difference between Froebel's kindergarten and the early kindergarten in Ontario related to the ages of the children involved. Froebel's kindergarten was a unit of child development, a bridge from the home to the school for children aged three to seven while the kindergarten in Ontario became a grade level beneath grade one and included mainly five-year-old children, although it was possible for children from ages four to six to attend.

For the most part Froebel's theories and practices were followed enthusiastically by the kindergartners in Ontario. Educators who grasped Froebel's doctrine of unity agreed that mankind was created in the image of God and, therefore, destined to live a productive life in harmony with Him. They agreed, too, that the aim of education was to bring the child up in the knowledge of God so the child could mature fully. Those who failed to grasp Froebel's doctrine of unity failed to recognize the significance of harmony and balance in education by development. They also failed to comprehend the breadth and all-inclusiveness of Froebel's aim. Certainly, other aims suggesting different priorities began to receive an equal emphasis.

Both humankind and nature were subject to God's laws, although these laws of growth and development could be seen more easily in nature than in mankind. One of these laws was that all living things grew from within outwardly, each according to its own type and uniqueness. The recognition and practice of such a principle made possible a depth development of the child from within outwardly, for these laws, which were God's laws, were active within the child and resulted not only in growth but led the child in the path of self-discipline and thus to a greater possible freedom.

Kindergartners agreed with Froebel that the child's first educator was the mother, and his first social experience was in the family. In addition, they felt that the kindergarten offered a wider social atmosphere to the child than was possible for the home to provide. For the sake of child development, kindergartners tried to bring the home and school into closer harmony through mothers' meetings.

The kindergarten was viewed by some educators as the foundation of the public school system. It was through a child's experiences in the kindergarten, nature walks and his play with concrete objects that the child formed impressions of his world as well as of God's operational laws. To the early kindergartners, as to Froebel, the child built the foundation for his future education with the impressions he was forming through his own experiences.

Child study was the new science which grew out of the New Education Movement and the Froebelian Kindergarten Movement. Froebel had urged educators to know their children, to listen to them and to observe them at play. Kindergartners were aware that they, too, needed to know a child if they were to help him towards his full development.

Froebel's curriculum was practiced by Ontario kindergartners. The curriculum was designed to lead the child into a full and harmonious development as well as to educate him in harmony with God, humankind and nature. Therefore, the content of Froebel's program and that of the early kindergarten was similar. However, it was not always possible for kindergartners to take the children on nature walks or to provide them with gardens and suitable pets and it was difficult for some to provide adequate substitutes for these activities. Froebel believed that the child by observing nature learned God's ways, and in caring for a garden and pets learned how to accept responsibility in partnership with the Creator.

There were educators who agreed with Froebel that the right method of educating the young child was to guide him in his play. Only by this method could the psychological aspects of learning, the child's experiences, be combined with the logical, the kindergartner's guidance. The active child was the growing child. Play was the mediator between himself and his world. In play the child imitated social life and life in nature and as he did so he gained impressions. Through his play he was able to harmonize his experiences within himself and, at the same time, to develop skills. The kindergartner was to guide the child in his play by means of timely suggestions expressed both in language and in song. The atmosphere of the

kindergarten was to be one of love and freedom and the child was protected from harm and danger.

Faced with large numbers of children in the kindergarten, however, kindergartners found that they could not give the child so much freedom as Froebel had suggested, nor did they have time to talk with each child about his play. So some kindergartners began using group lessons in which they directed the activity of the children. Whatever the reason for the directed lessons, such directed activity tended to become mechanical, losing much of the creative and joyous spirit which typified a true Froebelian kindergarten.

Ontario educators believed the Froebelian Gifts and Occupations provided the child with suitable equipment and materials to learn about his world and to express himself creatively. In Ontario the Gifts were wooden blocks rather than the soft, pliable ones Froebel had originally used. Therefore, their shapes could not be changed and this made it more difficult for the child to experience relationships. The routines of the play in the early kindergarten were similar to those Froebel had recommended. The child removed the box from the blocks in such a way that initially he saw the blocks as a unit and thus could begin to form plans for using them.

The early kindergarten, then, was similar to Froebel's own kindergarten in many respects. His theories and practices were followed, his curriculum was introduced and his play method advocated. His equipment and materials, the Gifts and

Occupations, were also used. Therefore, even though the large enrolment in kindergarten classes prevented the use of all Froebelian principles with an individual child, and even though there were educators who failed to comprehend Froebel's doctrine of unity as well as his method of education, the kindergarten introduced into Ontario was essentially Froebelian.

CHAPTER V

CHANGING EDUCATIONAL THEORY AND PRACTICE: THE TRANSITION YEARS, 1914 to 1939

B y 1914, the Froebelian kindergarten was established in Ontario. It was gaining recognition as the foundation of the public school system, even though its metaphysical bases and method of education were not always understood. Kindergartners were optimistic about the future of the Froebelian kindergarten in Ontario and little realized the challenges that would soon confront them.

During the years 1914 to 1939, strong influences were brought to bear which affected the shaping of the young kindergarten in Ontario. The influences came from four sources: the Kindergarten-Primary Movement which had developed in Ontario, Maria Montessori's work with young children in Rome, the formation of the Institute of Child Study at the University of Toronto and the thinking of the Reconstructionists in the United States who advocated free play. Influences from Montessori's work and the Institute of Child Study have increased since the years of this transitional period, which were, roughly, the years between the two World Wars. Even so, the changes during those years were sufficient to alter the future course of the kindergarten.

The Kindergarten-Primary Movement

The Kindergarten-Primary Movement was based on Froebel's thought that the child's development should be a continuous whole, from the past, in the present and on into the future. Although the kindergarten was meeting with acceptance as a foundation year for the public school grades, there was need for closer harmony between the kindergarten and first two primary grades in order to make the primary grades a part of the early childhood education unit as Froebel had intended. As early as 1889, Leontine Newcomb of Hamilton had discussed the need to harmonize the primary classes with the kindergarten. She suggested primary teachers would benefit considerably from a study of Froebel's theories.[1]

Transition work uniting the kindergarten and the primary grades began in London in 1894. Kindergarten directors whose classes were in the mornings began to assist in primary rooms during the afternoons. They taught such subjects as arithmetic and drawing and, where possible, adapted the kindergarten equipment and materials to the primary child. A number of years later, when J. H. Putman became Inspector of Public Schools in Ottawa, he recommended that kindergarten directors should teach sewing to grade school children in the afternoons. Some also became principals' assistants.

---

[1] Hamilton, *Minutes of the Proceedings of the Board of Education* , 1889, p. 55.

In 1897, the kindergartners at the OEA appointed a committee to discuss the relationship between the kindergarten and primary grades, but made no formal recommendations at that time. Again, in 1913, a Special Committee on Kindergarten Regulations and Courses of Study was formed. As a result of their discussions the members of the Committee recommended to the Minister of Education that a course be introduced into the Normal Schools which would combine kindergarten and primary education. The aim of the course was to unite the kindergarten with the primary grades.

The Department of Education acted upon the recommendations of the Committee. Clara Brenton was given a year's leave of absence from the London Board of Education in September of 1915 to organize the Kindergarten-Primary class at the Toronto Normal School. Lillian B. Harding, Elizabeth P. Cringan, M. Maude Watterworth and Mabel F. Hodgins were appointed instructors.

Once the training class was underway, it was offered during the summers as well as the winter months. Kindergartners were required to study for one summer in order to obtain a Kindergarten-Primary Certificate, while primary teachers were required to study over two summers.[2]

Boards throughout Ontario could decide which classes they wanted to introduce for their young children. They could choose a kindergarten, a kindergarten-primary class, both, or neither. The kindergarten-primary class differed from the kindergarten in that it was an all-day class. The program was a combination of the Grade One program and the kindergarten activities. Kindergarten equipment and materials were used in the kindergarten-primary classes but the three R's were also taught. Work and play each had their set place in the timetable. It came about that in areas where there were kindergartens, few kindergarten-primary classes were formed, but where there were no kindergartens, kindergarten-primary classes were often introduced in preference to the kindergarten.

Toronto planned to establish kindergarten-primary classes but found it difficult to do so when they had so many kindergartens. Instead, through discussion, a closer harmony between the kindergarten and primary was emphasized. Emma Duff, a member of a committee of the Toronto Board and a prominent Toronto kindergartner,[3] recommended the formation of a Childhood Department for children ages four to seven. It was to include the

_____

[2]An interim Kindergarten-Primary Certificate was made permanent after two years' successful teaching experience. The issuing of Kindergarten Directors' Certificates and those of Assistant Kindergartners was discontinued after 1929.

[3]Emma Duff was author of *Cargoes*, a book of stories for kindergarten children. Ada Marean Hughes considered her to be one of the finest kindergartners in Toronto (notation from Laura Lunde).

kindergarten, kindergarten-primary, and junior and senior first classes.[4] Although the suggestion met with approval, it was not acted upon.

During the 1930's many kindergarten-primary classes became "reading readiness" classes. These were classes for children who had attended kindergarten but who were not yet ready to participate in the grade one program. However, the term "kindergarten-primary" continued in use into the 1950's. At that time the grant for these classes was discontinued and they were classified instead as "slow grade ones".[5] They did serve, however, to bring to the attention of educators that some children take longer than others to build the foundation for their education.

The intention had been to make the kindergarten-primary class the door through which the kindergarten program and methodology would enter the primary grades, but it so happened that the opposite occurred. It became the means whereby primary education with its emphasis on the three R's and the traditional method of instruction and work came into the kindergarten! By the time the kindergarten-primary classes were discontinued, a number of kindergartens had adopted the kindergarten-primary program. Thus,

today, the kindergarten-primary curriculum may be recognized in kindergartens by the academic program and the emphasis on work as well as play.

What of the influence of the Kindergarten-Primary Movement itself on the kindergarten? The thought behind the movement was to bring the kindergarten and the primary into closer harmony as the first step in realizing Froebel's plan, that education of young children be a unified whole, continuous and without lapses, each stage building upon the preceding one. The idea, however, appeared to meet a premature end when the kindergarten-primary classes were discontinued. Nonetheless, the essential idea of the movement, the harmony of the child's first years in school, was not lost. It continued to live on under the new name of Early Childhood Education.

Maria Montessori's Influence in Ontario

In 1907, Maria Montessori (1870-1952) opened a school for children from ages three to six in a tenement district of Rome. It was called the *Casa dei Bambini* or the "Children's House" and the children attended the school all day. Montessori, a medical doctor, had worked with retarded children and had designed didactic apparatus which utilized the child's senses in the development of the intellect. She had adapted her apparatus to the needs of the children in the tenement district.

---

[4]Toronto, *Minutes of the Proceedings of the Public School Board* , 1926, Appendix, p. 1394.

[5]Ontario, *Report of the Minister of Education,* 1950, p. 20.

As well as subject content, her program included an emphasis on the formation of habits of personal care and good housekeeping. The children were taught to hang up their clothes, dust the furniture and water the plants. The furniture was small enough to enable the child to perform her tasks without adult assistance. The didactic apparatus included geometric insets, tablets, musical bells, sandpaper letters and numbers, and frames for lacing and buttoning. The apparatus could be used by a child independently. The Montessori timetable was flexible enough to allow the child time to pursue her own interests. She played outdoors part of the time on large climbing equipment and swings. At noon she ate a hot meal which the children themselves served, and afterward had an afternoon rest. There were similarities between Montessori's program and the one used in nursery schools.

By 1912, Maria Montessori's book, *The Montessori Method,* had been translated into English and published in the United States. Her system attracted a great deal of attention. S. A. Morgan, Principal of the Hamilton Normal School, was sent to the United States by the Ontario Department of Education to discuss her system with American educators. He reported the results of his discussions in a bulletin entitled, *The Montessori Method: An Exposition and Criticism,* which was issued by the Department of Education.[6]

In his booklet Morgan expressed the view that the Montessori system lacked an emphasis upon the harmony of life so important in the Froebelian kindergarten. He noted that Montessori stressed individual activities over social interaction. Much of the child's time was spent alone in isolated activity with the didactic apparatus. There was none of the spirit of social play in the Children's House so evident in the Froebelian kindergarten.

This difference in emphasis may have resulted from a difference in aim. Montessori claimed that the child was striving towards the independence of adulthood, and, thus, one day would eventually leave home. Morgan did not agree with Montessori. He felt that the young person in his struggle for maturity left home not to become independent, but to form another family unit. To Morgan, an individual's ultimate goal was not independence but rather social harmony.

Morgan had a further objection to the Montessori system. He agreed that the child might develop skills as she used the Montessori apparatus, but he did not feel the child would develop a corresponding understanding of the social significance or the moral worth of either the objects she handled or the skill she acquired.

Too often the work of education is inclined to make the mere acquisition of knowledge the complete process, in the ex-

---

[6]S. A. Morgan, *The Montessori Method: An Exposition and Criticism*, Ontario Department of Education Bulletin No. 1, Toronto: L. K. Cameron Printer, 1913.

pectation that thereby the individual will be perfected.[7]

He referred to the lack of oral language in the Children's House and yet noted that Montessori would teach reading and writing to a four-year-old child. Morgan claimed that both writing and reading required a background of experience, language and thought which could not be developed by apparatus alone. The child needed social contacts with others in order to develop the listening and speaking abilities in the use of language.

Morgan concluded his report by recommending that some of the Montessori apparatus might be adapted for use in Ontario schools. He also suggested to Ontario educators that they should develop more exercises in sense discrimination. However, his overall assessment was that what Ontario already had in the Froebelian kindergarten was much superior to the Montessori system.

Looking at the system as a whole, we have reached the conclusion that there is no reason why the child between the ages of three and five in a healthy social environment should be robbed of its superior social and spiritual influences for the doubtful benefits of the Children's House.[8]

The Montessori didactic apparatus was supplied to the Normal Schools for experimental purposes. Boards were also free to purchase it and to explore the system if they so desired. Clara Brenton reported some observations of the London kindergarten teachers.

In our study of the Montossori [sic] System continued throughout the year. . . we found that while this system is rich in suggestions to all students seeking a deeper insight into the child's needs, that it gives little opportunity for the development of the child's individuality.[9]

At the time, probably largely as a result of Dr. Morgan's criticisms for he was the spokesman of the Department of Education in this matter, Montessori's ideas had very little influence on the kindergarten in Ontario, even though her apparatus was used and her system studied. The Froebelian kindergarten had been accepted and it was considered superior to the Montessori system.

Since the 1950's attention has turned once again to the possibilities of the individualized Montessori activities and to the flexible timetable. The reawakened interest may have been due to the acceptance of free play into the Ontario kindergarten, for both individualized activities and a flexible

---

[7] *Ibid.*, p. 12.

[8] *Ibid.*, p. 71.

[9] London, *Annual Report, The Board of Education*, 1913, pp. 45-46.

timetable are useful in a free play program.[10]

The Influence of the Institute of Child Study, University of Toronto

In 1925, the Institute of Child Study at the University of Toronto was formed with Dr. W. E. Blatz as its first director. It was originally known as St. George's School for Child Study.[11] A nursery department was included as well as a kindergarten for four-and-a-half and five-year-olds and the elementary grades. The dual purpose of the Institute was to undertake research into child development and to offer courses for parents and others who were concerned with early childhood education.

The nursery school and kindergarten children attended the Institute for a full day. The program was similar to that of an English nursery school and has remained much the same over the years. The child was greeted and given a quick medical inspection when she arrived at the Institute. During the morning there were alternate periods of indoor activity and outdoor play where large equipment such as swings, slides and bicycles were used. The child ate a hot meal at noon and then in the afternoon rested on a cot for approximately an hour.[12] The orderly carrying out of routines was emphasized.

The idea of forming institutes for child study grew out of the Child Study Movement at the turn of the twentieth century. The United States was the first country to organize such institutes. The primary purpose in the American institutes was to study the child and then make the findings available to parents and educators. The Institute in Toronto was patterned on those in the United States.

The research at the Institute of Child Study [in Toronto] is a reflection of the pattern of the 1920's pervading such institutions on the continent. Its purpose was based on a humanitarian spirit, its subject matter became the child as he developed in his life settings, its approach the integrity of the scientific method.[13]

---

[10] For a discussion of the free play program and its acceptance into the Ontario kindergarten see pp. 78-81.

[11] During the 1950's, Windy Ridge Private School, which was also under Dr. Blatz's direction, became part of the Institute.

[12] See William E. Blatz, Dorothy Millichamp, and Margaret Fletcher, *Nursery Education, Theory and Practice*, New York: William Morrow and Co., 1935.

[13] Staff of the Institute of Child Study, *Twenty-five Years of Child Study at the Institute of Child Study, University of Toronto, 1926-1951*, editorial board chaired by Mary L. Northway, Toronto: University of Toronto Press, 1951, p. 53.

Since its founding in 1925 the Institute has undertaken studies relating to a number of different aspects of child development such as personality, social development, motor skills, intellectual development, creativity, moral judgment and mental health. Studies of the child's mental health have always been a major part of the work of the Institute.[14]

Dr. Blatz claimed a child's sense of security contributed towards her state of mental health. He noted that a child's emotions were aroused when she was faced with a new situation. The child was at once put into a position where she must either retreat or attack. If she attacked the new situation, she showed her willingness to accept a state of independent security. It was through such new experiences that she would develop skills and acquire assurance. Dr. Blatz thus reasoned, that in order for a child to arrive at a state of independent security she needed to be able to accept situations and feelings of insecurity.[15] Many teachers in the kindergarten were later to refer to the importance of a child's sense of security in her overall development.

The Institute has provided courses for parents, educators and others. The staff has always worked in close association with the parents of their children. Since 1946 short courses such as Discipline, Pre-School Learning, and Family Relationships have been offered by members of the staff at the Institute in a number of areas throughout the province. For many years students from the Primary Specialists' Course at the Toronto Teachers' College attended the Institute for one week of their academic year in order to observe in the nursery and kindergarten and also to take advantage of the lectures. Others, such as nurses, also have attended lectures at the Institute. As a result, it is difficult to know just how far-reaching the influence of the Institute has been.

The staff of the Institute has always believed nursery education to be very important.

Today the nursery school must be looked upon not as a charitable institution, nor as an expedient for increasing the number of mothers in industry, nor as a convenience for parents, but rather as a necessary adjunct to child care and training. There are many aides – the doctor, the dentist, the social-service worker – who assist parents to carry out their responsibilities; the nursery school is an additional aid for helping the mother and father to prepare their children for a democratic way of living. The nursery school is for neither the privileged nor the underprivi-

---

[14] The Canadian National Committee for Mental Hygiene was instrumental in the formation of St. George's School for Child Study. *Ibid.*, p. 27.

[15] William E. Blatz, *Understanding the Young Child*, Toronto: Clarke, Irwin & Co. Ltd., 1944, p. 167.

leged, but for both. The nursery school is not a luxury, it is a necessity.[16]

There is no question that the program of the nursery department of the Institute has had an influence upon the programs of private nursery schools as well as upon other programs of early education. For example, there is an emphasis in public junior kindergartens upon orderly routines. Also, members of the Institute staff have assisted in establishing day-care centres in various cities throughout the province. The influence of the Institute has extended even to Britain where, during the Second World War, members of the staff helped to organize nursery schools.

The Free Play Movement

It was during the 1920's that the American Free Play Movement began to have an influence upon the kindergarten in Ontario. At that time, there were two major criticisms directed against the kindergarten. Psychologists were critical of the Froebelian equipment and materials which utilized the child's fine muscles, claiming these fine muscle activities were unsuitable in child development. Secondly, there were accusations of rigid formality which denied a child opportunities for creative expression and self-activity.

Psychological studies, most of which were undertaken in the United States, had revealed that the child's large muscle development preceded her fine muscle co-ordination. As a result, psychologists and educators objected to the small muscle activities in the kindergarten. They objected to the Art Occupations of sewing and weaving, as well as the practice of having a child place the blocks of a Gift into squares marked on the top of a table. E. T. Slemon, Inspector of Public Schools in Ottawa, believed the fine handwork of the Froebelian kindergarten caused a child to become fatigued and expressed his opinion in favour of large muscle activity. Little thought was given to the fact that children needed both large muscle and small muscle activities for their full development. It became an either/or situation.

For a number of years Mary Macintyre had advocated that enlarged Froebelian Gifts should be used. They had already been introduced into many kindergartens. The larger cubes were two inches square, twice the size of the original ones. The boxes of the fifth and sixth Gifts were three times the size of the original Gift boxes. The child sat on the floor to play with her Gift. Gradually, larger papers were used for the Occupations, and by the 1930's large sheets of paper and big brushes were used for painting.

Other types of play equipment appeared in the kindergarten. Toys such as trains, puzzles and dolls were put out on the shelves. Picture books were made available. Some kindergartens had a playhouse for

---

[16]Staff of the Institute of Child Study, *op. cit.*, p. 26.

dramatic play. More large muscle equipment was also brought into the kindergarten. By 1922 all the kindergartens in London had teeter-totters and during the 1930's floor blocks were introduced into most kindergartens in Ontario.[17] Gradually, as these changes were effected, it became old-fashioned to use the Froebel Gifts and complementary Art Occupations.

The second criticism, aimed against formality in the Froebelian kindergarten, was mainly a criticism of the directed lessons used by a number of kindergarten teachers.[18] Possibly these teachers may not have understood Froebel's method or they may have had such large classes that they were not able to allow a child the freedom to play. In any case, they did direct the child's activity.

These kindergarten teachers controlled the child in the use of the Gifts, not only how to care for the box and the blocks but by stating formally how the pieces should be placed, hardly a play activity! The child was to copy the inventions of the kindergarten teacher. At the end of the lesson some were given time for free play with the

Gift. "I always felt when introducing a new gift," wrote a former kindergarten teacher, "we should have one formal lesson to show the children how the blocks could be used."[19]

There were kindergarten teachers who tried to remain true to the Froebelian method of play. Clara Brenton felt that the kindergarten teacher's responsibility was to guide the active child. "Learning by 'doing', not by 'being told' brings wisdom to child life, important now as well as at later stages of growth."[20] In 1926 members of a committee of the Toronto Board of Education declared, "The central idea of the Kindergarten, that is, development through self-activity rather than as a result of instruction – is fundamental to all true education...."[21]

Play had always been accepted as the chief activity of the child in the kindergarten, although the Froebelians advocated guiding the playing child. Free play was not a new idea. Both Jean Laidlaw of London and Mary Macintyre of the Toronto Normal School had warned the kindergartners of the dangers inherent in free play. To

---

[17]Patty Smith Hill felt the large floor blocks not only developed the child's large muscles but placed him in a situation in which he had to ask other children to help him, furthering his social development.

[18]Gradually, those who taught in kindergartens were referred to as kindergarten teachers rather than by the child development name of *kindergartner*.

[19]No footnotes are given for the comments made by retired kindergarten teachers. For a list of the retired kindergarten teachers who contributed to the study of the public school kindergarten in Ontario undertaken by the author in the 1960's (see Appendix, p. 148).

[20]London, *Annual Report of the Board of Education*, 1928, p. 37.

[21]Toronto, *Minutes of the Proceedings of the Public School Board*, 1926, pp. 1393-94.

true kindergartners the play spirit was all important. Their objective, as stated by a retired kindergarten teacher, was "to convert school into play, which according to Froebel is the child's most serious business". The Froebelian trained kindergarten teachers agreed that the child should be developed in accordance with God's laws so that she might develop inner sensitivity and self-control. They thought of play as being orderly and as having the direct purpose of aiding a child in her development. "In order to develop freedom we tried to have the child learn self-discipline – action, be able to meet emergencies. These qualities lead to freedom."

The free play advocates looked at play as an outlet for a child's energies. Kathleen Eardley of Ottawa referred to the advantages of free play. In an article which appeared in *The School* magazine in 1938, she claimed that in free play the children learned to play with one another, to share and to respect others. They also learned responsibility in the care of their toys. Furthermore, she believed the free play period gave the teacher an opportunity to work with an individual child.[22]

In 1929, Emma Duff placed before the kindergarten teachers at the OEA the three choices which, in her opinion, faced them. Their first possible choice was to accept the radical changes recommended by the American Reconstructionists and introduce free play into the kindergarten. The second

was to continue Froebel's practices with his concept of guided play. Thirdly, they could introduce the infant school idea and teach the three R's. Duff went on to refer to the "hopeless and lawless confusion" of the free play on the one hand, and the "rigid formalism" of the infant school on the other. To her, there was only one sound choice, and that was to continue the Froebelian kindergarten, but she would be true to its spirit.

> But I feel that it is possible to base one's practice on Froebel's principles, to use his materials according to his method and animated by his spirit, to accept anything new that is in harmony with these, and, by so doing, to steer a middle course, which is, in reality, more scientific and more sound pedagogically than either of the other types described.[23]

The influences which were brought to bear upon the kindergarten as well as the criticisms of psychologists and others, caused kindergarten teachers a great deal of concern. Many were uncertain about the future of the kindergarten if the changes were to be effected. They questioned what might happen if free play were introduced and there was no formality. Jean Care, a kindergarten teacher in Toronto, remembered their dilemma at that time. Claire Senior Burke, who instructed kindergarten-

---

[22]Kathleen E. Eardley, "The Free Play Period in the Kindergarten," *The School*, p. xxvii, 1938-39, p. 30.

[23]Emma L. Duff, "Essentials to Kindergarten Practice," *Ontario Educational Association. . .* , p. 106.

primary students at the Toronto Normal School for many years, claimed the Froebelian trained kindergarten teachers were also put on the defensive by criticisms from psychologists. Then, too, they had to defend themselves against attacks from educators who frowned upon formality in the kindergarten.

However, no decision was ever made by all the kindergarten teachers together. During the 1930's some simply started to discard the Gifts. They collected all the blocks in one large container and nailed down the lids of the large Gift boxes which they then painted to use as floor blocks. Both the small and large cubes and bricks as well as other toys were used by the children in free play. Meanwhile, students taking the kindergarten course at the Toronto Normal School up to the mid1930's continued to study the Gifts and Occupations as part of the equipment and material of the kindergarten.

Play as a method of education had been beset by misunderstanding and difficulties ever since it was first advocated by the early kindergartners. The difficulties to be overcome in making play understood as a method of education were further confounded when some teachers accepted free play and others did not. By the end of the transitional years several different practices were apparent in the Ontario kindergarten. A number of Froebelian trained kindergarten teachers still adhered to Froebelian theories and practices. However, as they retired, Froebelianism seemed to disappear. Other kindergarten teachers continued to value Froebelian theories but no longer supported the practices. As well, there were those in the kindergarten who supported free play and there were yet others who rejected all play in favour of directing the child's activity.

Summary

While the kindergarten retained something of its Froebelian theory, Froebelian practices were gradually eroded during these transitional years. Kindergarten-primary classes, as well as being the door by which the kindergarten program and methodology could enter the primary, proved to be a door for the three R's, and the idea that young children should learn to work as well as play, to enter the kindergarten. Montessori's ideas were not accepted in the Ontario kindergarten at first because educators considered the Froebelian kindergarten to be better for the child in terms of all round child development than the Montessori system. But once free play had been accepted into the kindergarten, teachers became interested in the individualized activities of the Montessori system and the idea of a flexible timetable. The influence of the Institute of Child Study has increased with the years through its research and teaching programs. Modern teachers discuss the importance of a child's sense of security to his overall development. They also emphasize the need for orderly routines, particularly teachers in junior kindergartens.

When some of the kindergarten teachers accepted free play into the kindergarten, another method of education was introduced, and the challenge of making guided play understood as the method of education, became even greater. Some kindergarten teachers continued to guide the child's play according to the Froebelian tradition, some provided opportunities for free play and other's chose to direct the child's activity. By the 1940's, the kindergarten had attained a new level of maturity, but conflicting ideas were leading to further confusion amongst both educators and parents.

CHAPTER VI

CONTINUED GROWTH OF EARLY CHILDHOOD EDUCATION IN ONTARIO, 1939 TO 1967

The period from 1939 up to 1967, Canada's centennial year, was characterized by two trends; the growing harmony of kindergarten education with the primary grades and the extension of early childhood education first downwards to include the three and four-year-old child, and then in breadth, to include the rural school child. Junior kindergartens were introduced into Ontario schools in the 1940's. Kindergartens for rural school children were included in the new central schools as they were built. The growing harmony in early childhood education was to be seen in the new teacher training course, the departmental programs of study and the increased awareness on the part of educators and parents alike that the kindergarten is the mediator between the home and school.

The Primary Specialists' Course introduced in 1939 into the Toronto Teachers' College was one reflection of the growing harmony in early childhood education. Instead of separate courses for pre-school education and the grades, the course, which followed in the tradition of the kindergarten-primary idea, was expansive enough to include all classes from kindergarten to grade two. When junior kindergartens were introduced into the schools the course was extended to include the theory and practice of the junior kindergarten as well. The instructors appointed to teach the course at the Toronto Teachers' College in 1939 were Elsie A. Sherin, M. Maude Watterworth, and Claire Senior Burke. In 1966, the Primary Specialists' Course was also introduced into two other teachers' colleges, Ottawa and Hamilton.

During the late 1930's and early 1940's the public school, too, was undergoing a metamorphosis which was bringing it more into harmony with the kindergarten. In 1937, the Department of Education had undertaken a major revision of curricula from grades one to six. The emphasis in the revision was upon the child and the importance of his development. The Department, in urging teachers to utilize the child's activity in the learning process, advocated the Project Method. The new thrust complemented the kindergarten where the emphasis had always been upon the child and that he learn through his own activity.

The Departmental program of studies for the kindergarten was completed in 1944, but it was not merely intended for the five-year-old kindergarten. It included programs for the junior kindergarten, senior kindergarten and kindergarten-primary. Indeed, hope was expressed that the new kindergarten program of studies would also be of help to primary teachers.

It is the purpose of the following program to make provision for those entering school at the permissive ages of three and four as well as those entering at five; to integrate the work of the kindergarten and that of the regular grades; and to afford guidance to teachers of primary classes in schools where a kindergarten is not established.[1]

It was the first time that early childhood education in Ontario was presented officially as an integrated whole. The revision was a milestone in Ontario's educational history.

For a time, during the late 1950's and early 1960's, there was no Departmental program of studies for the kindergarten and the 1944 program was considered to be outdated. The Department issued a list of books concerning kindergarten education which were to be used by teachers as reference materials. It was during those years that a number of boards in Ontario undertook the compilation of their own program books. These local program books were not unalike. They were organized according to themes, and suggestions were given to the teacher for topics, stories, poems, songs, games, art and handwork.

It was during the 1960's that the Department once again undertook a review of the curricula, this time from the kindergarten through grade six. The new revision differed from the old in its organization. In the new program each subject was organized in a vertical arrangement from kindergarten through grade six rather than having all the subjects presented for each grade in a horizontal arrangement. One assumption underlying the revision was that a child in kindergarten would thus be presented with the basic concepts of each subject.

The Curriculum Branch of the Department of Education had endeavoured to build upon the best from previous courses of study. There were frequent references and quotes in the revisions during the 1960's to the revision of 1937. Certainly the aim of education was similar.

> The schools of Ontario exist for the purpose of preparing children to live in a democratic society that bases its way of life upon the Christian ideal.
> Such a society aims to provide the greatest possible opportunities for the self-realization, security, and certain basic freedoms, to maintain legal justice, to achieve economic justice, and to afford the individual opportunities to participate in all decisions affecting his welfare.[2]

Another aspect of the growing harmony in early childhood education was the emphasis on the kindergarten as mediator between the home and

---

[1] Ontario, Department of Education, *Program for Junior and Senior Kindergarten and Kindergarten Primary Classes of the Public and Separate Schools*, 1944, p. 8.

[2] Ontario, Department of Education, *Interim Revision, Introduction and Guide*, 1967, p. 2.

school. This mediatorial role of the kindergarten seemed to be recognized by educators and parents alike. The child felt "at home" in the kindergarten atmosphere and through his own activity and play was gradually introduced to the subject matter of the school. The 1944 Program of Studies referred to the "oneness" in a child's life which resulted from close parent-teacher relations. Mention was also made of the harmony necessary between the kindergarten and the rest of the school.

> This increasing co-operation between school and home is nowhere more clearly discernible than at kindergarten levels where the mother frequently conducts the child to and from school and where many occasions are found for consultation between teacher and parent as to the best means of achieving their common purpose.
> There likewise exists a need of more intimately articulating the kindergarten with the regular school system.[3]

This awareness of the unity between the home and school was a step toward the fulfillment of the Froebelian plan.

Teachers sought closer relations with parents through interviews, book-

lets and by other contacts. Kindergarten registration, which took place in the spring of the year previous to the child's attendance at kindergarten, was usually the first contact many parents had with the kindergarten teacher, except in cases where other children in the family had previously attended kindergarten.

It was during registration that booklets and information sheets were given to parents. These booklets referred to the benefits which the child would enjoy as a result of home and school cooperation. The kindergarten program was usually explained in the booklet and suggestions were made for ways in which parents could help their child with the learning process during the kindergarten year.

Parents were asked to record on a separate page special information about the child which was not included in the registration form nor on the medical card. Questions were asked about a child's knowledge of commonplace objects and events, for example. The information gained was of help to teachers in understanding the child, but this information sheet, where it was used, seemed to be optional.

Parent visits in the kindergarten and interviews between the teacher and parents were also arranged. In the spring, during Education Week, many parents visited the schools. As well time was scheduled for parent-teacher interviews throughout the kindergarten term. Teachers found the interview helpful in becoming acquainted with the child's background. It was most

---

[3] Ontario, Department of Education, *Program for Junior and Senior Kindergarten. . .*, 1944, p. 6.

helpful, however, if proper preparations were made.

> I feel there should be concern, thought, and planning between teacher and parents for the welfare of the child. Interviews, if properly held, can further this cause.[4]

A number of teachers sent newsletters home with the children in order to inform parents of the current happenings in the kindergarten and to explain the program. Some teachers also requested help from parents with parties or excursions. In these ways teachers hoped they would better relations between home and kindergarten and thus further each child's development.

There was yet another aspect of the kindergarten as the mediator between the home and school. The kindergarten provided the child with at least a year in which he could build a foundation for his formal education. As far as program was concerned there seemed to be general agreement that school subjects should be introduced to the child during the kindergarten year. When the school curriculum was revised in 1937, the aim and method of the school were brought into closer harmony with the theory and practice of the kindergarten. Thus, the kindergarten, at that time, did become

more truly a foundation for the school grades.[5]

In the 1950 Report of the Hope Commission a reference was made to the dual function of the kindergarten. On the one hand, the members of the Commission considered kindergarten training a worthwhile supplement to home training while, on the other, they expressed the opinion that the kindergarten was the most suitable setting for a child to be prepared for the elementary grades.

> There can be no doubt that kindergarten training serves a most useful purpose in supplementing home training, in assisting the child in the transition from home to school life, and that it helps progress and achievement throughout the regular grades.[6]

In 1939, 14,982 children were attending kindergartens in Ontario and 8,063 children were attending kindergarten-primary classes.[7] The number of children attending kindergartens has increased considerably since 1939. During the 1950's,

---

[4] No footnotes are given for comments made by teachers. For a list of teachers interviewed by the author during the 1960's (see Appendix, p. 148).

[5] A consideration of the kindergarten as the foundation of the school combines both child development and the curriculum which is *education by development*.

[6] Ontario, *Report of the Royal Commission of Education*, Toronto: Baptist Johnston, 1950, pp. 53-54.

[7] Ontario, Department of Education, *Report of the Minister, 1939*, p. 121.

however, the kindergarten-primary classes, as such, were discontinued and junior kindergartens were introduced into the province during the 1940's. By 1967 there were 97,557 children attending kindergartens and 3,736 children attending junior kindergartens.[8] These statistics also include the figures for the rural school children who attended kindergartens in the new central schools.

Junior Kindergartens

The first kindergartens for children aged three and four were introduced into the Ottawa schools during the school year of 1943 to 1944. Dr. McGregor Easson, Chief Inspector of Schools in Ottawa at that time, claimed that the decision of the Ottawa Public School Board to introduce kindergartens for three and four-year-old children had been influenced by the benefits which children had received in both British and American nursery schools. Dr. Easson suggested that the school had the opportunity to provide a better environment for the child for a few hours each day than it was possible for a mother to arrange in the home. Toronto introduced their first junior kindergarten classes four years later, in 1947. The number of classes in both Ottawa and Toronto has gradually increased since that time.

The program for junior kindergarten was similar to that of the half-day nursery school. The child would undergo a quick medical inspection when he arrived at the class each day. He could then choose a toy with which to play. In addition to free play the children enjoyed group games, interpreted rhythms, sang songs and listened to stories. Time was scheduled for outdoor play with large equipment such as wagons and tricycles. During the half-day session the children were served a snack which consisted of juice, a cracker or a piece of fruit, and afterwards had a rest time on pads or blankets placed on the floor. The orderly execution of necessary routines was emphasized with the young children.

In Toronto, junior kindergartens were considered part of the child's developmental program which extended into the primary grades. In 1960 the Toronto Board undertook a research study of its junior kindergartens. The principal reason for the study was to investigate the value of junior kindergarten experience in the child's later school achievement.[9] The data collected included background information about the children, teachers' ratings and the results of tests — the Draw-a-Man Test and standardized tests of achievement, intelligence and creativity. At that time, however, it was difficult for the Research Department of the Toronto Board to make any assessment of the effect the child's junior kindergarten

---

[8]Ontario, Department of Education, *Report of the Minister*, 1967, pp. 62-63.

[9]*An Outline of a Longitudinal Study from Junior Kindergarten Through the Elementary Grades*, Research Report No. 23, Toronto: Board of Education, 1964.

experience had on later school achievement. Researchers found too many factors were involved. Most of the junior kindergartens, too, were located in the poorer districts of the city and this also made the interpretation of the data difficult.

While many educators agreed that junior kindergarten experience was beneficial, there were a number of practical considerations to be overcome, considerations such as cost, space and properly prepared teachers. Over the years the Institute of Child Study has encouraged the extension of junior kindergarten education. In 1950, the Hope Commission Report also referred to the advantages gained by a child from junior kindergarten experience. The writers of the report recommended that boards establish such classes but they realized that cost would probably be a delaying factor.

If local authorities have discharged their primary responsibility, they should, in our opinion, be encouraged to provide educational facilities for younger children.[10]

Kindergartens for the Rural School Child

A further inclusive development in early childhood education since the 1950's has been the provision of kindergartens for rural school children.

---

[10]Ontario, *Report of the Royal Commission* . . . , p. 53.

Kindergarten education was not feasible in rural areas where children attended a one-room rural school for grades one to eight. With the amalgamation of small boards into larger administrative units and the building of central schools, kindergartens were provided for rural school children. The parents of these children, as well as the trustees, felt that kindergarten would be a valuable social experience for the rural school child before he was challenged by the academic work of grade one. However, it was difficult to arrange transportation for the children when the kindergarten was a half-day session. It was a problem, but not an insurmountable one. In some areas parents organized car pools to transport the children at the noon hour. Some central schools offered an all-day kindergarten program having some children attending Monday, Wednesday and Friday, while others attended Tuesday and Thursday. The following week the children attended on the opposite days.

Summary

The kindergarten and the school began to move closer together during the late 1930's and early 1940's. The Primary Specialists' Course, which included special training for classes from the junior kindergarten to grade two, first introduced into the teachers' colleges in 1939, was an indication of that growing harmony. The curriculum revision of 1937 moved the school toward a closer harmony with the aims and purposes of the kindergarten. At that time, too, the Department of Education urged grade teachers to utilize the child's activity in his education, a method always used in the kindergarten. The 1944 program of studies for the kindergarten was a milestone in Ontario's educational history for it included programs for children in the junior kindergarten, senior kindergarten and kindergarten-primary. It also offered helpful suggestions to primary teachers. Thus, for the first time early childhood education was presented officially as a unified whole.

The kindergarten was recognized by parents and educators alike as the mediator between the home and the school. It combined a home-like atmosphere with the beginnings of the school subject matter. Parent-teacher relations were important in that concept. As well, the kindergarten with its play method now needed to be *accepted* as the foundation of the school system.

Early childhood education was extended downward throughout the years. Some three and four-year-old children were attending junior kindergartens. Many rural school children now had the opportunity to attend kindergarten. Thus, Ontario was moving closer to a fulfillment of Froebel's original plan, that the kindergarten be a unified whole pro-viding individual opportunities for harmonious education and development, and that all children from the ages of three to seven be included in a family grouping arrangement.

CHAPTER VII

EDUCATIONAL THEORY AND PRACTICE OF THE MID-CENTURY KINDERGARTEN

The kindergarten introduced into Ontario in the 1880's was essentially Froebelian; Froebelian theories and practices were advocated and Froebel's equipment and materials used. During the transitional years from 1914 to 1939 influences brought to bear upon the kindergarten led to change. One outcome was that Froebelian equipment and materials were discarded and replaced by free play. Another was the interest in the individualized activities and flexible timetable of the Montessori system. Further, the academic program of the kindergarten-primary was introduced into some kindergartens.

What had the theories and practices of the kindergarten become by the 1960's? What was the metaphysical basis of the kindergarten or at least its aims? What were the views concerning child development and the curriculum as well as creativity? Which methods were used in the kindergarten, and what were the equipment and materials?[1] And finally, where had the kindergarten arrived in relation to the Froebelian

kindergarten that had been introduced into Ontario almost a century earlier?

Aims in the Kindergarten [2]

Aims suggested for the kindergarten by educators interviewed by the author related either to child development or to the curriculum.[3] Within these two categories of aims, three received considerable attention; the total development of the child, the social development of the child and the preparation of the child for grade one. Kindergarten and primary supervisors were inclined to stress the aim of total child development. This aim was also mentioned in all the program books. Teachers, however, referred more to the child's social development and to her readiness for grade one than to her total development. Then, too, educators were only in agreement about the aim that the child be prepared in the kindergarten for grade one; they did not agree on how this could best be accomplished.

Claire Burke of the Toronto Teachers' College believed that the child should live fully each day. To her, education was a process of development and information was of

---

[1] The author travelled throughout Ontario during the academic year of 1965 to 1966 talking with supervisors, inspectors and retired teachers. Many of the quotes in this chapter relate to those conversations as well as to letters received.

[2] Metaphysics used here as a heading would be misleading. In conversation with kindergarten teachers, the author found teachers spoke of "aims". At that time, there did not seem to be a recognized metaphysical basis for the kindergarten in Ontario.

[3] For a list of the aims suggested by teachers and other educators, see Table 1, p. 91.

secondary importance. When she was teaching her students she frequently referred to the words of Edna Dean Baker, "He who lives the life of the present day of his development most fully will be most ready for to-morrow."[4]

The two aims of social development and preparation of the child for grade one seemed to co-exist in the minds of many kindergarten teachers. However, teachers who stressed these aims usually changed their emphasis during the kindergarten year. The child's social development took precedence over other aims during the first three months of the term. Teachers felt that in the months from September to the end of December a child needed to develop acceptable habits of group behaviour. When the term began again in January, the aim was altered from the child's social development to preparation for grade one.

The aims mentioned by teachers will be more fully discussed in the next section entitled *Views of Child Development and the Curriculum*. There was very little, if anything, said about a common philosophy. The trend in thinking seeemed to be toward the eclectic. It is also necessary to keep in mind that the program itself is an aim because the program only offers a plan for child development and recommends the subject matter a child should learn.

---

[4] Interview with Claire Senior Burke, October 13, 1965. (Edna Dean Baker was a prominent American kindergartner.)

However, there is no guarantee that every child will be fully developed or learn what she should. As one teacher wrote, "I feel a kindergarten teacher's life is made up of 'we hope', 'I think', 'we attempt', when it comes to aims and goals in the kindergarten." In turn, it should also be remembered that method is the complement of aim, for by the right method an aim is realized.

TABLE I

AIMS OF KINDERGARTEN TEACHERS AND KINDERGARTEN-PRIMARY SUPERVISORS IN ONTARIO, 1965-1966

The aims referred to both child development and the curriculum. The first aim listed was mentioned most frequently, and the last, the least number of times.

Teachers and supervisors desire that the child:

be socially developed
be totally developed
be ready for grade one
have a broad program
have facility in the language arts

learn to listen
be curious
learn to follow directions
be independent
develop good work habits

think and reason
have confidence
develop good attitudes
be introduced to the subject

matter of the school
develop physically

develop skills
enjoy kindergarten
become responsible citizens
feel secure
adjust to life in school

be honest
accept responsibility
have an inquiring mind
be interested in his world
develop self-control

have good manners
gain knowledge
formulate concepts
develop powers of observation
know one's self

develop acceptable behaviour patterns
be creative
appreciate art and music

Views of Child Development and the Curriculum

The development of the whole child has always been important to kindergarten educators. In 1950 the Report of the Hope Commission drew attention to the emphasis there has always been upon the child in kindergarten education.

> Froebelianism stood for the "child centred" school, and for growth through creative and expressive activity. On this continent, especially, it led to a new concept of education as a process concerned with every aspect of the pupil's growth to

maturity or, as it came to be phrased, with the development of the whole child.[5]

Collectively, educators, when discussing the development of the whole child, usually referred to her physical, social, emotional, intellectual and spiritual development. It was possible, however, that an educator would not always mention all those aspects of child development. Such an example is given by a teacher from Peterborough who heartily agreed with the *Ottawa Kindergarten Guide Book:*

> Educators agree on the importance of providing stimuli and appropriate environments for the physical, emotional and intellectual development of the young child. We feel that it is also an important part of the kindergarten teacher's work to provide suitable experience for the child's spiritual nature.

Teachers were becoming more aware of their need to be knowledgeable about child study and felt they had benefited from studies undertaken in both Britain and the United States. They agreed that they should be aware of the general needs of the children, needs common to both urban and rural children. They also needed to be familiar with the individual needs of a child, her background, her home and the socio-economic status of

---

[5]Ontario, *Report of the Royal Commission on Education in Ontario*, Toronto: Baptist Johnston, 1950, p. 35.

her family. To know each child was an absolute necessity if they were to assess her abilities and work towards furthering her development.

Growth remained a watchword of the kindergarten. Teachers claimed the kindergarten child could only achieve her fullest development through her own growing. One teacher wrote, "I try to meet the child as an individual wherever he is – to try and see the world from his point of view – and then encourage him to grow as fully as possible." Claire Burke of the Toronto Teachers' College always placed the emphasis upon the child's striving, not upon the results of that striving. To her, as to Ada Hughes in the early days, the child's effort was essential to personal growth.

The atmosphere and environment of the kindergarten were also to be conducive to child growth and development. In the 1966 interim report for the kindergarten, the Department of Education emphasized the importance of atmosphere. Reference was made to the need every child had to feel loved and accepted if she were ever to attain her full development.[6] The report also recommended that the environment should be structured to provide a wide variety of experiences for the child.

In their attempt to provide a kindergarten setting which would promote child development, boards

---

[6]Ontario, Department of Education, *Kindergarten*, 1966, p. 6.

tried to have no more than 30 children in a kindergarten. Even with a group as large as that, teachers tried to find some time during the half-day session to work with one child or a small group of the children.

Educators in the 1960's truly accepted the kindergarten as the foundation of the school system. They were aware of two important considerations in building the foundation; first, the intangibles of character development and, second, the child's development of an initial understanding of school subjects. Burke emphasized the development of intangibles within the child; such traits as thoughtfulness,truthfulness, courage, and dependability. Teachers discussed the development of the child's attitudes quite freely. They wanted her to cooperate with school authorities and to develop a liking for school. Teachers were also anxious that a child would begin to understand the school subjects.

That educators considered the kindergarten year a preparatory year for grade one was indicated in such statements as the following:

By the time the child completes the kindergarten he should be ready to take his place in grade one and cope with all the new experiences planned for his particular program.

Educators accepted the value of the kindergarten year but differed over what constituted the "best" kindergarten program in order to prepare a child for grade one. One group advocated the full development of a child within a broad program. To quote from the Ottawa *Kindergarten Guide Book* of the 1960's,

> Kindergarten should not be considered merely a preparation for first grade but rather an experience in purposeful, successful living and learning. The preparation for Grade One is the happy by-product.[7]

Another group of teachers emphasized a readiness program. They attempted to provide the child with reading readiness skills of visual and auditory discrimination, number readiness skills and pre-printing skills. There was a third group who tried to steer a middle course. Those teachers combined a broad program with the teaching of readiness. They tried to give the child many experiences as well as allow her time for free play, but they also took the time to develop readiness skills.

The program in the kindergarten encouraged the children to be active. The activities could include free play, discussion, rhythms, songs and games, art or handwork, readiness activities and stories. Teachers felt it was easier to hold the interest of the children if the activities were short. Some kindergartens also had three routines, "lunch" which consisted of milk, crackers, fruit or juice, a recess and a rest.

There were teachers who used a block timetable. According to the block timetable, similar activities took place within one period of time. The timespan might last anywhere from 40 minutes to an hour. The first block included such group activities as discussions, singing and rhythmic movement, while the second time block was devoted to individualized activities. These blocks of activities might also be in the reverse order. Whichever timetable was used, the kindergarten session usually closed in the traditional manner, with either a discussion or a story.

There was a strong desire among educators to further child development through the curriculum and, as well, to inculcate in the child the beginnings of the school subjects. A statement in 1946 in an article written by Evelyn Murray, a Toronto kindergarten teacher, reveals what was still the purpose of the kindergarten. "A good kindergarten program is well-balanced, challenging, progressive, and is designed to develop the whole child."[8] Educators felt the program should become increasingly more complex over a year. Yet, it should be flexible enough to meet the needs of the immature child as well as to provide a challenge for the more mature child. As one teacher wrote, "We need a program which meets both the mature child and the younger child, where both find enjoyment and satisfaction."

---

[7] Ottawa, *Kindergarten Guide Book*, p. 1.

[8] Evelyn Murray, "The Child in the Kindergarten," *The School*, XXXV (November 1946), p. 116.

Emotional Development

Words used most frequently by teachers when discussing the child's emotional development were "security" and "success". Teachers tried to develop a sense of security within the child when she first entered the kindergarten, by helping her to feel she was an important member of the group. Experiences which developed the child's skills also added to her feelings of security, for in doing things for herself she became more confident.

Educators believed that the child who felt secure and who experienced success would likely be a happy child, and they agreed that every child in kindergarten should be happy. As one teacher wrote, "I want children to be happy in school and enjoy the whole experience." Some teachers expressed the opinion that the underlying reason for happy children in the kindergarten was a teacher who taught with her heart as well as with her head.

Spiritual Development

Few teachers commented on the child's spiritual development, but those who did believed that the knowledge of God's love gave depth and breadth to child development. They agreed that a child who was aware of God's love usually acquired desirable social graces, was sensitive to others and, as well, developed a healthy spirit of independence. Claire Burke believed that the knowledge of God as the source of all good gave the child a sense of security and, therefore, contributed to her emotional stability.

Teachers agreed, however, that Christianity was best taught by example. By taking an interest in all that concerned the child, the teacher also reflected God's love.

Most educators linked spiritual development with character development and this, they felt, was primarily a family responsibility. Yet, they did not feel they could ignore any aspect of child development. There was some agreement of the view that the school should support the home in its religious teaching and character training but never try to supplant it. Honesty was mentioned frequently as a worthwhile character trait to be developed in the child.

Social Development

Teachers considered the child's social development to be of major importance. For most children the kindergarten would be their first social experience outside the home. Some teachers expressed the view that the child's social development was an important part of her training for responsible citizenship. They believed that responsible citizenship was a necessary aim of education in Canada where the way of life is based upon the democratic system. To them, even the patterns of social cooperation which were developed in the kindergarten were significant.

Teachers recognized that the four and five-year-old child is egocentric. Therefore, they planned a number of group activities in the kindergarten such as singing, singing games, stories and discussions in order to draw the children together into a group relationship. Free play also offered many opportunities for social interaction. For example, in free play the child learned the importance of sharing and taking turns, as well as to respect the rights of others. Teachers believed the child also learned to shoulder her share of responsibility in taking out and putting away the toys and materials the children used.

Those involved in rural education were aware of the importance of the social experience for the children in the kindergarten. A child at home might be lonely, having no playmates other than brothers and sisters, some of whom might be away at school all day. Educators felt it only right that rural children should have an equal opportunity with urban children and that the child from a rural community should also have the benefits of the social experience in the kindergarten before being required to meet all the demands of the grade one program.

Social Studies

Teachers felt the child's understanding of the world around her, as a prelude to the study of history and geography in the school grades, was best developed through activity. As the children interacted with one another, habits of social co-operation leading to good citizenship were emphasized. Such activities as dramatic plays, games and excursions were planned for the child. Ideas which related to social life and work were often conveyed through stories and songs. The child also

enjoyed having visitors in the kindergarten and a great deal was made of holidays, birthdays and special events. Often teachers would arrange programs for festive days. In most kindergartens there was a Christmas Closing to which parents were invited. For a number of years a dramatization of the Christmas Story, written by Claire Burke, was used in many Toronto kindergartens as well as throughout the province. London also held a Flower Festival each spring.

Physical Development

The child's physical well being was important to educators. Arrangements were made for the child to have a medical examination, either by the family physician or the school doctor when she was registered in the spring for kindergarten in the fall. Some boards also arranged to have the child's hearing and vision tested, although that was not usually done until the following May or June. The public health nurse recorded the results of the child's physical examinations, her immunization against communicable diseases, and any illnesses she might have contracted. Teachers, aware that a young child tired easily and was, therefore, more susceptible to illness, tried to plan alternate periods of vigorous activity and restful occupation in the kindergarten.

The development of the child's senses was also considered important. Teachers mentioned the five senses of sight, taste, touch, hearing and smell in discussion but in practice more experiences were planned which stimulated the senses of sight, hearing and touch than of taste and smell. Burke, who supported this Froebelian view of sense training, referred frequently to the use of the senses in developing the child's intellect. For example, it was through the senses that a child formed impressions in mathematics of proportion, size and number.

Physical Education

Educators tried to plan the physical education program to meet individual needs. While teachers believed the child should be given some tasks which required fine muscle co-ordination, the emphasis in the kindergarten during the 1960's was on the child's large muscle development. Most of the physical activities took place in the kindergarten room but teachers also arranged to take the children into the school gymnasium at least once a week so that the children could have more freedom of movement and use some of the large gym equipment. Much of the physical movement in the kindergarten room was in connection with the singing games and rhythms.[9] When planning the physical education program teachers took into consideration that girls seem to mature more quickly than boys.

Science

Science, like social studies, was also an activity program. The child was to observe natural phenomena and make her own discoveries. She was encouraged to conduct experiments with the equipment available in the kindergarten room. Suitable equipment such as a weighing scale, magnets and seasonal objects were usually placed at the science centre. That the child's participation in the science program was emphasized over her acquisition of factual knowledge was illustrated in a statement from the *Kindergarten Program* of the Mississauga Board of Education. "In the Kindergarten we are concerned with experience in science processes rather than the acquisition of facts."[10]

Teachers tried to provide many experiences for the child. There were pets such as guinea pigs and rabbits in kindergarten rooms. Teachers found that the children enjoyed watching living things such as tadpoles growing into frogs or eggs in an incubator hatching into chicks. The children also planted seeds in a planter and watched them sprout. Children not only enjoyed actual experiences but they learned more from their own observations than they did from merely being told about events. Educators agreed that it was through experiences with nature's materials that a child became aware of the wonders around her.

---

[9]Rhythms help develop the child's muscular coordination but they are also creative expressions.

---

[10]Mississauga, *Kindergarten Program*, p. 25.

Language Development

Language development received an important emphasis in the kindergarten program. Educators agreed that while the child gained impressions of the environment through her experiences, language was important to her understanding of those experiences. Therefore, the language experience approach of listening, speaking, printing and reading received a great deal of attention during the 1960's in Ontario, although few five-year-old kindergartens included printing and reading in their programs.

In the kindergarten the child was given opportunities to express herself as well as to listen. A great many stories and poems were used – Bible stories, nursery rhymes and fairy tales, as well as stories of everyday events, occupations and social life. Teachers encouraged the child to compose stories and rhymes of her own. A child was given opportunities to express herself in conversations and discussions, during the daily news or in "Show and Tell" where the child brought an object from home to "show" to the other children and to "tell" them what to her were its most interesting characteristics. Teachers were anxious that a kindergarten child should learn to express clearly both her ideas and her feelings.

It was important to kindergarten teachers that vocabulary be related to experience. For the most part, teachers tried to use words that would be easily understood by a child but they realized it was also important that new words be presented. One expressed that view in this way.

We must learn the language of the kindergarten child and adapt our questioning and choice of vocabulary way down to this level – but at the same time presenting new vocabulary as may be meaningful and challenging.

Most teachers considered printing and reading to be grade one subjects. Thus the greatest emphasis in the kindergarten of the 1960's was on readiness for these activities. However, teachers did not agree as to what constituted the best readiness program. One group of teachers believed that the best preparation for a child was a broad program with many experiences, many opportunities for both listening and speaking and with a wide choice of art media. They felt the art activities developed the child's fine muscular coordination in preparation for printing.

Another group of teachers emphasized skills. They had the child draw lines and shapes in order for her to be prepared to print in grade one. They concentrated on exercises which gave to the children considerable repetition in visual and auditory discrimination. By this means they felt that the child would be able to see differences and similarities in shapes of letters and words and to hear and distinguish sounds at the beginning of words. In both programs the child usually learned to print her name. A library centre with its display of picture books was considered an important part of any reading readiness program.

Some teachers, by informal means, encouraged a child to read. The child became acquainted with the printed symbol through experience charts and labels which were attached to objects around the room. At that time there was a very small group of teachers who actually taught reading and printing in the kindergarten. These teachers had a formal reading lesson where the child used word drills and was given a pre-primer to read. Their classes resembled the former kindergarten-primary classrooms.

Intellectual Development

Intellectual development is closely associated with a child's language development. Teachers agreed that the child's intellect was developed to a large extent by her experiences, and that those experiences became clear to her through language. Teachers wanted each child to become observant and to learn to listen. One teacher wrote, "Those who listen usually do well." Good questioning on the part of the teacher was also considered a way of drawing out the child as well as a way to stimulate her mind. Thus, good questioning would nourish the child's intellectual development.

Educators believed more attention should be paid to the development of the young child's reasoning powers and they believed that problem solving developed these reasoning powers. The child was to ask for the teacher's assistance only if that assistance were truly necessary. Some educators were anxious that a child form basic concepts of subject matter. In order to do so, however, a child needed to be at a stage where she could classify information and see relationships. The development of the young child's reasoning power has been receiving increasing attention over the years. In the 1960's many educators felt that the intellectual capacity of a child was being underestimated.

Mathematics

Basically, a child would begin to understand mathematical ideas from handling concrete objects. Suitable incidental experiences in the kindergarten environment also furthered her understandings as she became familiar with number, size, weight and money values. The child developed a number vocabulary, learned to count by rote as well as rationally and began to understand ideas of time and space. Numerals were sometimes used separately from concrete objects but there was very little abstract number work in the kindergarten. Where boards had adopted the New Mathematics program, one-to-one correspondence and grouping were stressed in the kindergarten. The shapes of the objects used in the New Mathematics resembled those of the Froebelian Gifts.

Music and Art

Teachers believed music and art to be creative, emotional experiences for the child. Both singing and rhythms afforded a child opportunities for self-expression. Furthermore, songs helped the child to understand her environment whereas rhythmic movement developed her large muscle coordination. Teachers found that children responded well to the musical programs in the kindergarten. A kindergarten teacher wrote of her experience,

I find music and rhythms excellent. Children learn quickly anything that can be sung or acted to music. Music is perfect for restoring discipline, relaxing children at rest period or letting them give vent to their feelings when they come to school in a frustrated or angry mood.

Music entered into the kindergarten program in a number of ways. The children played rhythm band instruments, sometimes under the teacher's direction and sometimes during the free play period. There were pianos in most kindergartens but teachers also used other instruments such as a drum for background in the rhythmic activities. Piano chords were considered preferable to verbal directions when the teacher wanted the children to change their activity. As well, appropriate recordings were used in music appreciation.

Art activities included crayoning, paper folding, cutting and pasting, modelling, stitchery, painting, wood gluing, paint printing, parquetry and the making of texture pictures. While teachers considered art to be primarily a creative activity, they also were aware that it developed the child's eye-hand co-ordination. Some teachers believed that a child could not be creative unless there was an outward stimulation to be so. These teachers attempted to motivate the child through stories or special experiences. Some used the handwork of the art program to teach the child to follow directions.

Claire Burke followed in the Froebelian tradition of creative expression. To her, art afforded the child an opportunity to express her inward thoughts in a visible shape. She claimed that the child benefitted most, not from producing a finished art product but from her striving and sustained effort. Other educators agreed with her. "What happens to the child during the art lesson is of far greater importance than the piece of art."[11]

Views of Creativity

Teachers believed creativity to be an expression of the inner child and, therefore, important to the child's emotional development. They agreed that the child's creativity could be expressed in many different ways; for example, in art, music, language, rhythms, play and mental activity.

---

[11] Mississauga, *Kindergarten Program*, p. 28.

They encouraged a child to compose her own songs and stories.

Teachers recognized that if a child were to be creative, she must have freedom. One teacher wrote, "An atmosphere of freedom within limits recognized by the child helps develop creative ability." A number of educators believed the informal kindergarten program and the flexible timetable offered the child many opportunities for creative expression. However, there were a number of teachers who felt they could give the child sufficient freedom for self-expression during the art activity or play period.

The equipment and materials available to a child also influenced her creative expression. One teacher wrote that the child needed "a variety of suitable equipment and materials to express himself creatively". Educators recognized that it was as a child exercised creative ability that she developed skills. In turn, skills made the child more confident and thus she became more creative within the environment.

A child needed to be encouraged by her parents and teachers alike if she were to develop confidence in the ability to express herself creatively. Teachers agreed that it was helpful if they, too, were creative because then the child could be "caught up with the joys and fascinations of new concepts and ideas".

Methods in the Kindergarten

During the 1960's there were at least three methods of education being used. The three methods were *guidance of the child's activity, directing the child's actions* and *free play. To guide* means "to advise" or "to lead", whereas *to direct* has the connotation of telling the child what to do. Those who practiced the former followed in the Froebelian tradition and guided the child in her self-activity, whereas those teachers who directed the children's activities planned and set out for them what was to be done. In free play the child played on her own or with others with the toys and other equipment. In addition, a number of educators at that time held the view that "work" should be a part of the kindergarten program.

Those who followed in the Froebelian tradition guided the child's self-activity by means of timely suggestions. The environment was a carefully planned one. Claire Burke believed the child should be free in her self-activity, but felt that she also needed gentle guidance. Other teachers agreed. One wrote of the way in which she perceived her role:

> Literally, a teacher does not teach; she guides a process inherent in the child which would go on even if she were not present but which should go on even more effectively if she is present.

Directed lessons were common in many kindergartens, especially in relation to handwork and the "readiness" subjects of reading, printing and arithmetic. In a directed lesson the child might be original in her expression, but she carried out the plan of the teacher. The teachers who used this type of readiness lesson sometimes gave the child a stencil to complete in order to see whether or not she had grasped the content of the lesson taught.

There were many educators in the kindergarten who supported the idea of free play. They advocated a structured environment where the furniture, equipment, materials and interest centres were planned to attract the children and to stimulate them to experiment with the various things in the room. The three most common interest centres in kindergartens were the playhouse, the library and the science centre. The program was developed, to a large extent, around the interests of the children, and the teacher exercised control through environmental factors. For example, four children were permitted to make up a family unit in the playhouse or there was only enough equipment for three children at the science centre.

No matter which method was used – guidance, direction or free play – there was a daily activity period in all kindergartens when the children played comparatively freely. The activity period could extend anywhere from 15 minutes to an hour, according to the value the teacher placed on free play. During the activity period each day, teachers encouraged a child who tended to choose the same activity to seek new experiences by choosing equipment and materials with which the child was not familiar. Most of the teachers tried to talk with individual children during that time and offer help where it was needed. The teachers felt they gained insights into individual needs and interests of the children during this activity period.

Teachers tried to create an atmosphere in the kindergarten which gave to the child both a sense of security and a sense of freedom. They felt such an atmosphere supported the child emotionally while enabling her to feel free to pursue her own interests. Burke claimed that a child needed freedom to make mistakes if she were ever to be properly educated. A comment from one of the teachers will illustrate the type of atmosphere for which they strove.

> The environment should be relaxed, sympathetic and secure. The child will not be afraid to make mistakes, he will be free to follow his own interests.

Teachers spoke of the rules in the kindergarten as the routines. The London Board defined a routine as "an orderly response that has become habit through repeated practice". That was a commonly accepted definition. Therefore, teachers in general agreed that routines should be few and very clear. Burke believed that just and sensible routines which aided in the organization of the kindergarten were important. Too many rules or too strict a discipline, however, could cause one child to become passive or another to rebel.

Routines were planned to ensure the safety of the children, to develop in them good housekeeping habits, to set the limits in free play and to provide for the care of the equipment and materials. For the most part, teachers decided on the routines but some did plan them with the children. A teacher wrote, "I find if the pupils set the standards and make the rules, they follow them much better."

The child in the kindergarten of the 1960's, then, enjoyed an atmosphere of security and freedom. Her needs were provided for in the equipment and materials especially chosen for her, and she was permitted to be active within the framework of the routines. She might have been guided by suggestions, directed in her activity, or she may have been allowed to play freely. But, whichever method was used by the teachers, they all maintained that the kindergarten child learns best through her own activity. To "learn by doing" was still a prominent motto of the kindergarten.

Play and Work

Educators agreed that play was essential to the child's development. They recognized that play was the natural expression of the young child and also that she learned best about her world through play. Teachers also found that they, in turn, learned a great deal about the child from watching her at play. While many educators agreed that play was essential to a child's development, quite a number feared that the child would never adjust to the work involved in the school grades if she did not learn to work in the kindergarten as well as to play. The separation of work and play became very apparent in statements made both by educators and by parents. A common remark related to the difference that existed between the play activities in the kindergarten and the work required in grade one. As one parent expressed it, "The kindergarten is play and then the children are thrust into the hard world of learning in grade one."

In order to overcome this difficulty, many teachers in the kindergarten tried to divide their programs into work and play activities. The free activity period (sometimes referred to as "playtime") and all the games were referred to as play activities, although teachers also used games to develop physical skills, number abilities and reading readiness skills of auditory and visual discrimination. Other activities such as art or handwork, readiness seatwork and reading were referred to as work (sometimes called "worktime").

There were, however, educators who realized that play really is the forerunner of work. They believed that play challenged the young child in many of the same ways in which work challenges the adult. A child who was totally involved in her play experienced the same joy that an adult might later find in creative work.

Some teachers were able to enter into the spirit of play with their children. In this way the teacher felt she could become more sensitive to the needs of each child and discover just when and how to extend her understandings.

Teachers did desire that each child learn and practice self-control in play. They agreed that a passive child needed encouragement to take part in activities whereas an aggressive child needed to learn to cooperate with the group. Burke, along with other educators, claimed the best way to discipline a kindergarten child who was a troublemaker was to isolate her from the other children.

It is obvious that methods of kindergarten education have been influenced by the American idea of free play. The Reconstructionists in the early 1900's who advocated free play believed that a child by nature was good and, therefore, within a structured environment all her choices would be good. Froebel, too, believed that the child was good. However, he differed from the Reconstructionists in that he believed a child should also be developed in harmonious relationships. For that to happen the child needed individual guidance, especially if she were to develop the necessary self discipline and sense of responsiblity.

Many educators in Ontario had difficulty in accepting the idea of an educational practice based on the view that a child by nature is good. Therefore, many teachers in the 1960's expressed reservations about allowing the child to play freely. Perhaps this was why free play was limited to one block of time in the half day kindergarten session. Dr. J. G. Althouse, in a speech at the Centenary of the Toronto Normal School in 1947, made this point of view very clear.

American theories of psychology and particularly the philosophy of John Dewey have exerted a deep influence on our educational thought and practice, but American Progressivism has never led the principals and staffs of our Normal Schools to believe or teach that whatever is natural to the child must therefore be wholesome. Our Normal Schools have held firmly to the faith that the individual is a social being, that his life is meaningless except in a social setting – in other words, that he must develop into a citizen as well as into a personality.[12]

Kindergarten Equipment and Materials

Educators were in agreement that the equipment and materials chosen for the kindergarten should help to further each child's development.

It is essential, therefore, that the classroom should provide a variety of materials and learning centres to encourage and

---

[12]Dr. J. G. Althouse, "Centenary Address," *The Toronto Normal School, 1847-1947* , Toronto: Printed by School of Graphic Arts, 1947, pp. 18-19.

challenge each child at his own stage of development.[13]

Teachers hoped that the play with the toys and games would help the child feel at home and at the same time introduce her to the subject matter of the school.

The kindergarten equipment and materials included both concrete objects and semi-abstract materials. There were toys such as trains, trucks, cars and airplanes. There were beads for stringing, pegs and peg boards and puzzles. There were number games, reading readiness games and games of skill. The materials, for the most part, were those used in art and handwork. Semi-abstract materials used included experience charts, stencils and workbooks.

Large muscle development was considered important, so jungle gyms, sand tables, carpentry benches and tools, equipment for water play, large balls and ropes were in evidence. Other possible pieces of equipment were teetertotters, wagons and pedal toys. These were certainly available in junior kindergartens.

There were pianos, record players and radios in most kindergartens because music had continued to have an important place in the program. A variety of visual aids including projectors and television sets were also available to teachers and children.

---

[13]Ontario, Department of Education, *Kindergarten*, 1966, p. 17.

Teachers emphasized certain routines in the use and care of the equipment and materials. The child learned where to find each object, where she could play or paint and how to put the equipment and materials away. Furniture appropriate to the child's size enabled her to be independent when selecting toys and art materials. Teachers hoped that each child would develop orderly habits and learn to share in the common responsibilities.

Summary

The kindergarten, which included children from ages four to six, was the mediator between the home and school. The three most common aims were child development, social development and the preparation of the child for grade one. Major differences within the kindergarten depended, to a large extent, upon differences in teachers' aims.

The kindergarten was considered the foundation of the school system. It was characterized by an emphasis on total child development – physical, intellectual, spiritual, emotional and social; and by an educational emphasis in which the beginnings of the school subjects were presented to the child.

Child development and education were accomplished through activity. Methods used by teachers included guidance, the directing of a child's activity and free play. The program, as well as equipment and materials were chosen for the purpose of developing the child and inculcating in her the beginnings of the school subjects.

CHAPTER VIII

THE EMERGING PATTERN

*I*n what ways, then, did the kindergarten of the 1960's in Ontario resemble or differ from the essentially Froebelian kindergarten introduced during the 1880's into the Ontario Public School System? By attempting to answer this question, we begin to see the developmental pattern of early childhood education in Ontario. It should not be surprising if the early kindergarten and the one in the 1960's bear marked similarities, for one is rooted in the other.

Similarities Between the Historical and Mid-Century Kindergarten

Aims

The kindergarten holds an intermediary position between the home and school. The early kindergartners spoke of it as a bridge between the home and school; on the one hand, they promoted mothers' meetings to improve the relationship between the kindergarten and the home and, on the other, they attempted to lay the foundations for a child's future education. Teachers in the 1960's also worked to improve teacher-parent relations. The aim of preparing a child for grade one was only part of the larger purpose of the kindergarten which traditionally was to help the child build a foundation for his education.

Another common aim of kindergarten educators was the development of the whole child. Early kindergartners spoke of the child's physical, intellectual and spiritual development while later educators also included social and emotional development when they discussed the whole child.

Child Development and the Curriculum

A watchword of the Froebelian kindergarten was "growth". The kindergartners believed that a child grew from within and that the purpose of the curriculum was to develop the child. Therefore, the early kindergartners studied the child in order to adapt the curriculum to his needs. The kindergarten teachers agreed that the child's growth was from within. They, too, desired that the curriculum develop the child.[1] Over the years advances made in child study have led to many insights into child development and education. Thus, kindergarten teachers have been able to develop a broad understanding of the young child and his education.

The atmosphere of the Froebelian kindergarten was a loving one. Kindergartners were encouraged to protect the child from harmful influences and yet to allow him

---

[1] In order to clarify the comparison of the early kindergarten with the kindergarten of the 1960's, educators from the early years are called "kindergartners" while those of the 1960's are referred to as "kindergarten teachers".

sufficient freedom for self-activity and creativity. They were also encouraged to give each child individual guidance. The difficulty that faced the early kindergartner was that she had a very large class of children. It was next to impossible for her to give each child the freedom and attention he required.

The atmosphere in the kindergarten of the 1960's had a different emphasis. Kindergarten teachers wanted children to be happy and secure, as well as to experience success. Most boards limited the number of children in a kindergarten to 30. Ideally, this was to make it possible for the teacher to allow each child a degree of freedom and to give each one some individual attention.

To the early kindergartners the Christian influence extended from the home into the kindergarten. The initial setting was the love within the family. In the kindergarten Christianity was taught primarily by example, but also through nature and the teaching of Bible stories. The child was encouraged to live out his Christianity in good deeds.

In the kindergarten of the 1960's, character development received the emphasis, although educators spoke of it in terms of Christian morality. Kindergarten teachers felt that both Christian teaching and character development were primarily a family responsibility. However, many believed that the public school should complement the training given in the home.

The curriculum of the early kindergarten was similar in its overall content to that of the later kindergarten, but differences existed within. In the Froebelian kindergarten, the child who cared for plants and animals did so that he might learn to accept responsibility. James Hughes claimed that it was in giving nurture that the child learned to act in partnership with God. The kindergarten teacher did not intentionally use the care of plants and animals to develop a sense of responsibility in the child. Her emphasis, instead, was more scientific, being placed on the child's observations, experiments and discoveries of natural phenomena.

Reading was not taught to four and five-year-old children in the early kindergarten. Kindergartners believed that the child at that age should first learn through his own play with concrete objects. It was through activity and play with the *actual* and the *real* that the child formed impressions of his world. Reading was considered to be a visual activity when the child was still at an age where he was "ear-minded".

Reading was taught in very few kindergartens in the 1960's but the readiness program was common. Some kindergarten teachers felt they could prepare a child for grade one by emphasizing readiness skills. Therefore, skills of auditory and visual discrimination were practiced and in printing readiness, the exercising of the child's fine muscle coordination by means of various drills, received attention. There were other kindergarten teachers who provided a broad program with many opportunities for listening and speaking. While most of the equipment in the kindergarten consisted of concrete objects, some teachers had introduced semi-abstract materials such as experience charts, stencils, and workbooks.

There was a logical sequence of development in the Froebelian Gifts. The child was guided in his experience from the known and simple to what he did not know and what was complex, but during the play the kindergartner returned again to the familiar, known and simple. In these ways the child saw each play as a total experience. The child was also helped to integrate new experiences with the old, as well as encouraged to discover relationships, especially between one experience and another, and certainly always to find meaning for himself.

James L. Hughes and his wife, Ada Marean Hughes, who followed Froebel's views very closely, claimed that a child's education should be *psychological* in terms of the child's experience and, as well, *logical* in that the kindergartner gave the child appropriate guidance throughout the experience. The child's first contact with his world was through his own activity, as putting forth of his energy, and thus he gained impressions of things. The kindergartner helped him to see relationships within the activity and to organize his thoughts in a logical way.

Many teachers in the kindergarten of the 1960's stressed the psychological aspects of learning during the free play time but failed to guide each child in logical habits of thought. Free play provided an opportunity for the child to be active in the environment, but it was difficult for the kindergarten teacher to find sufficient time to interact with each one in order to help the child organize his thoughts logically. In many cases, therefore, the children were left with unrelated, incidental experiences.

The art program of the 1960 kindergarten was more open than the program in the early kindergarten. The child was free to experiment with both the art media and the content. In the early kindergarten the Occupations used in the art program were a complement to the play with the Gifts so there was more structure in the early art activities. They included crayoning, painting, paper folding, sewing, cutting and pasting, weaving, twining or braiding, peas work and modelling. Their use depended on which Gift was used in play. The child made *forms of life* (things relating to everyday happenings), *forms of knowledge* (number stories), and created patterns of design or *forms of beauty*. Kindergarten teachers used materials similar to those of the early Occupations, only in freer ways. Their art activities also included such things as stitchery, wood gluing, paint printing, parquetry and texture pictures.

Creativity

Kindergarten teachers agreed with Froebelian kindergartners that creativity was an expression of the inner person. Ada Hughes stressed the importance of the child's effort in his creative endeavours. She believed that it was in striving, not in the results of that striving, that the child received the most benefit. Through the years there have been educators who agreed with Ada Hughes, educators who stressed the child's efforts over the result produced by that effort. Both the early kindergartners and kindergarten teachers heartily agreed that a child needed encouragement with his creative efforts.

Method

There was some similarity between the early kindergartners and later teachers with respect to methods of education used in the kindergarten. Kindergartners advocated guidance of the child's play but there were those who chose instead to direct the child's activity. In the guidance method, the child was given freedom to express himself in play. In directed activity, the plan was usually the teacher's. Early kindergartners may have known that they should guide the child in his activity, but found this difficult to do with such large classes of children. By the 1960's there were kindergarten teachers who recommended guiding the child's play but there were also those who directed the child's activity as some of the early kindergartners had once done. As well, there were kindergarten teachers who approved of free play within a structured environment.

The method of education chosen appeared to be closely related to the educator's concept of the nature of the child. To James Hughes, a child had potential for both goodness and badness and, therefore, needed guidance to bring out the good and to prevent bad qualities from growing within him. Dr. Hughes claimed that a child should be made aware that he, along with the rest of God's creation, was subject to God's order. The recognition and acceptance of God's principles by the child was the basis for his development of self-discipline.[2] The exponents of free play based their method on the view that a child's nature was good, and that the structured environment would influence the child to choose the good. To them, self-discipline developed through the social interaction with other children. However, throughout the years many educators in Ontario have had difficulty in accepting an educational practice based on the view that a child by nature is good.

Equipment and Materials

The Gifts and Occupations were the play equipment and materials of the early Froebelian kindergarten. The Gifts, which resembled fundamental shapes in nature, gave the playing child opportunities to form impressions of the world and its natural laws. The Art Occupations provided the child with complementary materials for creative expression. They enabled him to convey in creative ways the impressions he was forming within.

---

[2]Principles for living harmoniously with others include such qualities as kindness, patience, self-control, endurance, etc. See the *Bible,* I Corinthians 13: 1-13.

Most of a child's experiences in the kindergarten of the 1960's were with concrete objects such as toys, puzzles and floor blocks, although some kindergarten teachers included stencils and workbooks. The equipment and materials chosen were larger and more varied than they had been in the early Froebelian kindergarten. As well, special equipment such as climbing frames or swings were provided to encourage the child's large muscle development.

Differences Between the Early and Later Kindergarten

There were two major differences between the kindergarten of the 1960's and the Froebelian kindergarten introduced in the 1880's into Ontario. The first was the profound difference Froebel's philosophical concept of unity made to the early kindergarten and the second related to the Froebelian method of education, the guidance of the child's play.

The Froebelian View of Unity

The Froebelian view of unity permeated every aspect of the early kindergarten. In essence, the meaning behind the idea was that one could find the harmony of all life in God. Thus, the aim in the Froebelian kindergarten was Christian, to bring the child into a relationship with God so that he or she might find at an early age the harmony of life and be able to grow and develop within that harmony. It also brought to light the possible depth of child development within the harmony of family love as well as God's love. Furthermore, the curriculum needed to be sufficiently broad to include the knowledge of God, humankind and nature.

Early educators accepted Froebel's all-inclusive aim. James L. Hughes spoke of the need to lead the child to God and then to develop him in harmony with God that he, too, might use his energies for good purposes. In the 1960's many aims were suggested for kindergarten education. Most of them were concerned with child development and the curriculum, but there was no "umbrella" aim suggested for the kindergarten.

To the early kindergartners a child who was brought into his right relationship with God developed harmoniously from within -- physically, intellectually and spiritually. They spoke of the *harmonious development* of the *hand, head* and *heart.* The senses were the doors to the inner child. Froebelian plays were designed to develop the child in depth. Kindergarten teachers discussed the development of the whole child, but in their program planning did not seem to coordinate the indissoluble relationship between the various aspects of the child's development. For example, an activity might be planned to develop the child's physical skills while a different one was planned to develop his reasoning powers. The Froebelian kindergartners were able to use the same activity to develop the child physically, mentally and spiritually.

There was also an outer harmony of God, humankind and nature. The child who responded to God's love and acknowledged His laws developed in harmony with all of His creation. Such a child gained an understanding of God's ways, too, by observing nature, and in social relations of family and community he experienced God's love. In knowing God, then, he came to understand the laws of development evident in the natural creation.

These natural laws were not restricting; in fact, they provided for a greater freedom of growth. To James Hughes the child should be free in his development, but he needed to realize that he, too, along with all of creation, was subject to these laws. It was the God-likeness in the child that was to be given free expression. The child would then use his energies and creative abilities for good purposes. It was in recognizing and accepting God's laws within himself that the child learned to exercise self-control.

That the kindergarten was considered the bridge between the home and school was another aspect of Froebel's view of unity. The loving atmosphere of the home was brought into the kindergarten and the child, by means of his natural play, continued to learn about his world. Kindergartners organized mothers' meetings for the purpose of discussing Froebelian ideas with them. They hoped that together they could provide the child with a unified home and kindergarten experience.

The harmony of life found in God was also basic to social relationships. The early kindergartners accepted the Christian position that God was the Father of all, and thus all people were brothers and sisters. The child, therefore, was to be developed within the harmony of love - of God and in all the social relationships within the family and community.

Related experiences were essential to the child's understanding of the harmony of life. The child was never to play aimlessly, never to be given anything in isolation nor was he to be left without being helped to understand his experiences. The kindergartner in her interaction with the child was to guide him by means of her language and song. Thus she could help the child become aware of relationships within each experience, of the relationship of one experience to another and especially of the meaning of that experience to himself.

The child revealed his likeness to his Creator in his creative expression. Creativity, like self-activity, was spiritual energy. The child who had experienced God's love was able to give to others in creative deeds of love, life and light. As well, both music and art were considered creative expressions of the child.

Educators were inspired by Froebel's vision for the kindergarten. They understood the tremendous significance of his view of unity in child development and education. However, the Froebelian view of unity received less and less attention over the years and eventually was all but lost to the kindergarten. The kindergarten today needs to be aware once again of its rich Froebelian heritage, to understand anew the unifying aim of the Froebelian curriculum and to plumb the depths of child development which are possible when a child is developed within the wholesome context of love and harmony.

Guiding the Child's Play

Play is natural to a young child. It is both his self-activity and creative expression. Froebel organized the traditional plays of childhood into kindergarten activities in order to use them for each child's development and education. It was through play that a child developed in depth, in harmony from within himself and in all his relationships.

An essential idea of play practiced by early kindergartners was not to limit play to a set time on the timetable. *Play was the spirit of the kindergarten.* Jean Laidlaw of London claimed that the spirit of Froebelian play was similar to the joy an adult found in his work. Every activity of the children and kindergartner was to radiate that spirit of joy.

To the Froebelians, play was the mediator between the child and his world. In play with the Gifts and Art Occupations as well as in all the other plays of the Froebelian kindergarten, the child gained impressions of the world. Through the interaction of child and kindergartner, the kindergartner was able to help the child form clear and accurate impressions by means of her language and song.

In order for the child to benefit fully from the Froebelian plays, he needed freedom of movement as well as protection from harm and danger. It was only after the child had opportunities to express himself that he could be guided in his play. To direct the child's activity detracted from the spirit of joy in the play and therefore made the activity of little use in the child's development. Capricious or aimless plays of a child left without guidance dissipated his energies and often resulted in feelings of boredom.

By 1914, however, kinder-gartners in Ontario realized that they were failing to make Froebel's idea of play understood as a method of education. When free play was introduced into Ontario kindergartens during the 1920's and '30's, Froebel's concept of play became even more muddled. In many cases, too, free play was limited to a period of time in the kindergarten program. The Froebelian kindergartners had not limited guided play to any one time ; they believed the spirit of play should dominate all of the program. To add to the confusion that already existed, the idea that children in kindergarten should work as well as play was introduced with the kindergarten-primary classes! In view of the misunderstandings surrounding Froebel's play method, it should not be surprising that during the 1960's Froebel's method of guided play was used by so few kindergarten teachers.

Summary

The summary for this chapter is presented in the form of a table. The similarities and differences of the early Froebelian kindergarten introduced into Ontario with the kindergarten of the 1960's are highlighted.

TABLE 2

Similarities and Differences Between the Froebelian Kindergarten Introduced into Ontario and the Mid-Century Kindergarten

	Froebelian Kindergarten	Present Kindergarten
Metaphysic		
The Froebelian view of unity....	x	-
Aims		
to bring up the child in harmony with God.	x	-
to develop the whole child	x	-
with greater emphasis on social development	-	x
to help the child build a foundation for his education	x	*
to prepare the child for Grade One	*	x
Child Development and the Curriculum		
growth of the child from within	x	x
study the child in order to suit the curriculum to his needs	x	x
curriculum concerned with God, humankind and nature	x	x
a program chosen to give variety of experience	-	x
a readiness program	-	x
foundations laid by means of the child's impressions	x	x
foundations in readiness activities	-	x
foundations laid in basic concepts of subject matter	-	x
Creativity		
the child is creative because he is created in the image of God....	x	*
creativity is an expression of the inner child	x	x
the child's effort is most important in the process	x	x
Methods		
to guide the child's play	x	*
to direct his activity	x	x
to introduce a free play period	-	x
Equipment and Materials		
concrete objects	x	x
semi-abstract materials	-	x

*The asterisk, where it occurs in a column, indicates that *some* rather than a majority of educators agreed with the statement.

CHAPTER IX

OBSERVATIONS AND IMPLICATIONS

*I*t is important now to draw together the major observations resulting from a comparison of the early Froebelian kindergarten with the kindergarten of the 1960's and to consider the implications of those observations for the continuing development of the kindergarten in Ontario.

Some Observations

The early Froebelian kindergarten and its more modern counterpart were found to be similar in several ways. The purpose of the kindergarten had remained the same; it was still considered to be the mediator between the home and school. Early kindergartners as well as kindergarten teachers were in agreement that the kindergarten not only united the home with the school, but it also provided a foundation for the child at the beginning of his formal education. Primary supervisors and some kindergarten teachers agreed with early kindergartners in their aim of total child development but there were also kindergarten teachers who placed a good deal of emphasis upon the child's social development.

Kindergarten teachers were in agreement with early kindergartners that child study was of the utmost importance and that the curriculum existed for the purpose of child development. There was more

emphasis in the early kindergarten upon developing a loving atmosphere than there was in the 1960's. The kindergarten teachers expressed more concern than did the early kindergartners with building a child's sense of security and providing situations in which she would experience success. Both kindergartners and teachers agreed that a child developed from within herself and thus needed a certain amount of individual attention. The smaller classes of more recent years have made it possible for the teacher not only to give the child some of the attention she needs, but also to allow her a greater degree of freedom.

There was found to be general agreement on the type of program kindergarten children should have, but differences existed within the programs. Christian teaching, mainly by means of example, was emphasized more in the early kindergarten while kindergarten teachers of the 1960's tended to stress character development. They agreed with the early kindergartners, however, that the first responsibility in relation to religious training and character development remained with the home. There was also a difference in the science program. In the early kindergarten the child was to learn how to accept responsibility by caring for plants and animals. For the kindergarten of the 1960's the observation and discovery of natural phenomena received more attention.

There was a difference in attitude towards reading. There was no reading or formal reading readiness in the early kindergarten and, therefore, no semi-abstract materials were used. The child gained impressions from the concrete objects with which she played and from her other experiences. Impressions gained from concrete experiences provided the foundation for later formal learning. Although little reading was taught in the kindergarten of the 1960's, reading readiness was considered important. It was presented either by means of a broad program with a great deal of oral language and many types of art media, or through a more formal program which included the teaching of the reading readiness skills of auditory and visual discrimination. Where reading readiness was taught, semi-abstract materials were used.

There was also a difference in the art programs. In the 1960's kindergarten the art program was freer than it had been during the early years and there was also a wider choice of art media. In the early kindergarten the emphasis was placed on using the Art Occupations to complement the child's play with the Froebel Gifts.

Kindergartners and teachers agreed that creativity was an expression of the child's inner being. They agreed that the child's creative effort was of more value in her development than the product which resulted from that effort. Both would give the child a great deal of encouragement for creative effort.

The early Froebelian kindergarten and its more modern counterpart differed in two major ways: first of all, in the area of method and, secondly, in the attitude towards a metaphysical base

for the kindergarten. Very few kindergarten teachers used the Froebelian method. Early kindergartners who had grasped the meaning of Froebel's words attempted to nurture the child's development by guiding her play. Unfortunately, from the inception of the kindergarten in Ontario, there has been a misunderstanding of Froebel's method of guiding a child in her play. Froebel's play idea has been confused with two other activity methods, directing a child's activity and free play. Nevertheless, a few kindergarten teachers likened their role to that of a gardener and did use the true Froebelian method.

The second major difference between the early kindergarten and the way it had developed by the 1960's related to the metaphysical base. The Froebelian view of the unity of all things in God gave to the early kindergarten common principles which the kindergarten of the 1960's did not have.

Implications

The kindergarten has progressed considerably since it was first introduced into Ontario. There has been a steady growth in the areas of child study and child development, curriculum and creativity, but, unfortunately, this has not been the case in the areas of methodology and metaphysics. The two differences between the early kindergarten and the kindergarten of the 1960's bring to light two weaknesses in our modern day kindergarten. The methods used in kindergartens may be activity methods but they may not be all that beneficial in developing each child. Secondly, our kindergarten lacks a metaphysical basis. There needs to be a concentrated effort by educators to strengthen these two areas of kindergarten education in Ontario.

Is there anything to be learned from turning once again to the theory and practices of the early kindergarten, and even to go so far as to re-examine the Froebelian origins? Very definitely, yes. Froebel justly deserves to be called the *Father of Early Childhood Education*. He emphasized child development as well as the need to present the child with a curriculum which served to develop her in an allrounded way. As the founder of the kindergarten, he suggested it include children from ages three to seven years, for it was during those early years that the foundation of the child's education would be laid. It is sensible to study his method of kindergarten education in order to become aware of the benefits to childhood which are to be found in his philosophical view of unity.

The Play Method of Kindergarten Education

Childhood is the time for play. A healthy child plays so spontaneously that there is no doubt that she was born with the inner urge for such activity. This is as it should be, for play is of untold benefit to a child. It is an expression of the child's energy. Each child is developed as she plays and, because she is participating in life through her play, she is becoming familiar with her world. Is it not

obvious why Froebel claimed that educators should use play activity to further all aspects of a child's development?

A child is both self-active and creative in play. Play calls forth from her united and concentrated effort. Her powers of concentration are increased and she learns to sustain effort. This putting forth of effort, this exerting of energy on the part of the child as she plays, is vital for her all-round, healthy development.

A distinction needs to be made between the child's *self-activity* and her *activity*. In self-activity, the child conceives an idea, formulates a plan to carry through her idea and then executes the plan. Self-activity not only makes demands upon every capacity of the child, but the child, if she is to accomplish her plan, must exercise self-discipline and self-control.

Activity has a more generalized meaning. It includes activity which can be another's idea or plan. In other words, the activity is the child's own but the idea or plan or both may not be. Obviously, such activity does not make the demands upon the child that her own activity generates. The more an activity is the child's own – idea, plan and deed – the greater will be the development that takes place within the child.

There are kindergarten teachers who fear what might happen in a classroom where each child is free to plan and carry out her own idea. In their concern they overlook the simultaneous development of a child's self-discipline. Self-discipline needs to be developed along with self-activity.

Froebel's aim in education was to bring up a child within the harmony of God's love. He believed that a child who developed in a conscious awareness of that harmony developed into a responsible person. Such a child could not do what she pleased when she pleased. In recognizing herself to be God's child, she realized that she was subject to God's laws and one of those laws was the exercise of self-control. Furthermore, Froebel would nurture in the child qualities of kindness, sympathy and thoughtfulness toward others and all of creation. In Froebel's opinion, it was only in self-activity where the child exercised self-control that she revealed her likeness to her Creator.

It is through play that a child participates in life and begins to understand her world. In the kindergarten, play is the means by which the child and the curriculum come together. In her play the child harmonizes her new learning with what she already knows. She plays with concrete objects and imitates adult life and work as well as the life she sees in nature. Thus, through her own experience the child forms an ever increasing number of impressions.

A child is very happy as she plays. Happiness is, without a doubt, the outstanding characteristic of play. The early Froebelian kindergartners claimed that it was the child's happiness (they referred to it as *the spirit of joy*), which contributed the most to her development.

The kindergarten was *a garden of children* to Froebel, where each child grew and developed into what she had the potential to become in somewhat the same way plants flourished when tended and cultivated by a gardener. Child development began with the child's striving and effort. A child must do her own growing and learning; however, the role of the kindergartner should not be minimized.[1] She allows the child freedom to grow but she must possess certain professional abilities if she is to be the child's guide. She must have a knowledge of children as well as an understanding of each child in her care, she must be skillful in guiding each child towards a full development of her potential, and she must be wise enough to provide an atmosphere and a curriculum which will be conducive to child development.

If the kindergartner is to promote child development, she must study the child. She must observe her, particularly in her relationships with others, and she must interact with her. By listening to the child and observing her, she will become aware of her abilities and interests as well as her needs, and she will also discover what the child knows and does not know. In view of her increased understandings of the child, she can then plan experiences which will broaden her understandings

---

[1]"Kindergartner" is a more appropriate term than "teacher" for the one who guides the child, in view of Froebel's concept of his or her role as *a child nurturer*.

and help her to acquire further and new impressions.

The kindergartner's role as a guide is a challenging one. She must protect the child from harmful influences, yet at the same time, not restrict her freedom unduly. She guides the child in her play but she must be careful not to interfere with her, for if she does, she will likely weaken her power of action. Neither must she remain so aloof from a child's play that it becomes aimless, for then the child's education is left to chance and she will likely become bored or restless. Furthermore, she must be very perceptive of each child and his or her needs if she truly is to serve as the children's guide.

If a child is to be developed and to form clear and accurate impressions through play, the kindergartner, as well as listening, must gently guide the child by means of language and song. It is through language, literature, poetry, drama and the songs and singing games which accompany a child's play that her experiences truly become meaningful to her and the impressions made upon her become clear and accurate. In such ways, the kindergartner can help to bring the psychological and logical aspects of kindergarten education into harmony within each child.

Furthermore, the child needs to be guided by the kindergartner if what is good within her is to be nurtured and if destructive tendencies are to be prevented from growing. As the gardener permits only good plants, not weeds to grow in her garden, the kindergartner should nurture in the child all that is good. If rudeness, bad manners and disrespect for others were always recognized for what they are, they would not be allowed continual free expression. To Froebel, who believed that the child should be developed in harmony with God, it was the positive and good qualities that were to be encouraged and given free expression.

A child also needs guidance so that the freedom she enjoys in her play does not give self-centred and selfish qualities opportunities for growth. For example, will negative traits and habits develop in the child who is always allowed to follow her own interests for as long a period as she chooses? Will such a child become self-centred and eventually a slave to her own whims? It is wise to keep in mind that each child needs a balance in her education, and needs to be guided in her development within the context of the whole, whether it be within the family, the kindergarten or the community.

The kindergartner then has a responsibility to provide an atmosphere conducive to child development as well as a curriculum designed for that purpose. The curriculum includes equipment and materials, the objects with which the child plays. Therefore, they should be selected with the utmost care.

Kindergarten teachers have a wide choice of options in both equipment and materials. It would be helpful if more research were undertaken to discover to what extent the equipment and materials in use in kindergartens are furthering child development. Essentially, the worth of equipment and materials to the kindergarten child depends upon the use she makes of each piece, but it would be helpful to know, even in a general way, possible effects upon the child of the equipment and materials with which she plays.

There are two essential guidelines to be followed if the child's play is to be meaningful. First of all, it is necessary to provide the child with the type of equipment and materials that give her ample opportunities for self-activity and creative expression. Secondly, the equipment chosen should be concrete, not abstract nor even semi-abstract, because the child is to be given ample opportunities to form impressions of her world through her play.

There is a sequential pattern in the Froebelian Gifts which helps children to see and understand relationships. This was especially true of Froebel's own Gifts which were made of soft materials such as vegetables so that the child could change their forms. Furthermore, the child could recreate her world in microcosm with the various objects that made up the Gifts. The Froebelian materials, the Art Occupations, offered to the child further practical and complementary experiences with ideas suggested in play with the Gifts. It would be wise to reconsider the advantages of the Froebelian Gifts and of using the Art Occupations in complementary ways.

Froebel's words, *Come, let us live in harmony with our children*, are still applicable. Not only does each child benefit from a close association with adults, but the kindergartner, because she is with the children, begins to understand them both as a group and individually. Therefore, she can plan further experiences which will be meaningful for her children as well as each child. It is as the kindergartner enters into the spirit of the play, becoming part of its ebb and flow, that she has the opportunities to guide each child.

If every kindergartner had a clear understanding of the role that play could have in the child's development and knew how to guide her by timely suggestions both in language and song, the kindergarten experience would become much more meaningful for each child. Educators in Ontario need to be aware of the actual value of free play, to realize the dangers inherent in directing the child's activity and to consider once again Froebel's view of play with his concept of the kindergartner as the child's guide.

The Metaphysical Basis of Unity for Kindergarten Education

The second major difference between the early and the later kindergarten was that the early kindergarten had a metaphysical basis, while the latter had nothing comparable. In Froebel's view a philosophical base for kindergarten education was absolutely essential. To Froebel, the foundation of life as well as of education was found within the harmony of God's love. Within the context of that love a child was to be developed fully in all of her relationships to God, humankind and nature. In being rightly related to the Creator and his creation, the child experienced the harmony of life which only love can give.

It needs to be clearly stated that Froebel did not intend that the harmony of which he wrote be interpreted as conformity, for he saw both unity and diversity in life. Those things which were different, when they fulfilled their individual roles in the scheme of things, contributed to the unity of life, for in God all things are united; all things originate from him, are sustained by him and return to him.

The child could experience the harmony of life only if she grew up to know and keep the laws inherent in the universe; laws of growth and development, of order and of self-discipline. They were not confining rules but rather life-giving guidelines, freeing the child for purposeful and creative activity. Thus, even the natural laws were another evidence of God's care.

Many educators and others consider that the foundations of a child's life are laid by the time she is seven years old. The child can spend possibly three of those years in the kindergarten and the first two primary grades, but foundations are laid in the home long before the child ever enters the kindergarten. Froebel recognized the harmony that is possible in a child's life when home and school are united in their attitude towards child development. The child moves steadily in continuous progress from home to

kindergarten within the circle of family love and the loving interest shown by the kindergartner. Thus the child can build a solid foundation for her future education. There is very definitely a need for parents and teachers, as well as other specialists concerned with the home and school, to work together so that the child's first seven years are a unit, a solid foundation for her life and education.

Froebel intended that his kindergarten include children from ages three to seven and that during those years the foundation be laid for the child's future education. The kinder-garten has long been considered a foundation year within the public school system and there has also been a growing harmony of the kindergarten with the first two primary grades. This pattern first became evident in the 1890's with the beginning of the Kindergarten-Primary Movement. Now that junior kindergartens are becoming part of the public school in Ontario, it is time to ensure that these first four years of a child's education are the foundation years. The arrangement should be one of family groupings where children are together from ages three to seven. There could be small groups of similar ages but together they would form a larger group. A team teaching type of ar-rangement would allow each child to move at her individual pace within that grouping and to build a solid foundation for her future education.

Most educators in Ontario plan for the child's education to extend from senior kindergarten to Grade Twelve. There will not likely be many more years before most educators discuss education in terms of junior kindergarten through college or university. One year in a kindergarten certainly does not give sufficient time in which to build a proper foundation that will support that educational structure. This is yet another reason why more thought needs to be given to the importance of building the child's foundation extending over the period of the first four or five years of education, from the junior kindergarten at age three or four to the end of grade two when a child is seven or eight.

Furthermore, there should be more educational centres available for the young child. The sociological need to provide care for young children remains. Mothers are working, more so than ever before. Even in situations where children are well cared for in the home, the educational need for which Froebel planned is there.

Kindergartens for children living in rural areas, a comparatively recent development, have been made possible with the building of consolidated schools. Transporting young children for a half-day program, however, remains a problem. Some communities have resolved the difficulty by having young children attend for a full day every other day.

The junior kindergarten idea is still new in Ontario and classes are not yet available to all children. Ottawa tries to include all four-year-old children but the youngest are excluded if there is crowding. In Toronto, junior kindergartens were established in the 1960's mostly for the disadvantaged child but in some cases for the children of new Canadians. Junior kindergarten classes for these particular children is a forward step but there is still a need to extend the kindergarten downward to include all young children.[2] Many parents, although they have a great love for their child or children, feel they lack expert knowledge and skill in matters of child rearing and development. They seek out the help of those who are professionally trained.

Froebel believed the foundation of the child's life and education was built primarily in love and, secondly, in the impressions the child was forming. It is important that the child, especially during the formative years, knows she is loved both by parents and kindergartners. Parental love and love from other adults is to the child a reflection of God's love. Such love can give the child an emotional stability which will remain with her throughout life. Froebelian kindergartners believed the nurture of the child's heart and sympathies as well as Christian teaching (which was mainly by example) were very necessary if the child were to build a solid foundation during her early years. However, they agreed, as do educators today, that the

---

[2] The early Froebelian kindergartner had morning kindergarten sessions only and visited in the homes during the afternoons. In this way she was able to discuss child development with the mothers. It might be helpful to initiate such a program for children who are considered disadvantaged as well as for the children of new Canadians. Time should be given to organizing and offering programs for these parents.

family has the strongest influence upon the child's development, and most certainly upon her emotional and spiritual development. The kindergartner, however, can complement the nurture given in the home, especially if she works together with the parents. Thus, it is very important that educators give considerable attention to how they attempt to build the child's educational foundation and with what attitudes, equipment, experiences, etc., they choose to build.

Secondly, Froebel believed that impressions which the child formed as a result of her self-activity were the basis of her understanding. There was to be no academic learning in the kindergarten, no second-hand knowledge. All that the child learned she acquired through her own play and experiences. A child forms impressions from all she is exposed to; in her play, from excursions and from nature walks. That these impressions, which she forms early in life, be of high quality is essential in building during these foundation years.

Impressions made at the beginning of life are frequently referred to in one of two ways; either they are likened to "the planting of seeds" which implies the cultivation and growth of the child's character and understandings, or they are likened to "the laying of foundations" which suggests a right base for the structure of the child's education. In any case, the implication is that the beginnings, while of great importance, are not easily seen. Froebel would build the child's educational foundation in love and with

the impressions the child is forming, neither of which can be seen.

Froebel also believed that if the child's impressions were to be of lasting value, she should be helped to see relationships. Nothing was to be given to her in isolation. This is yet another aspect of Froebel's view of unity. The kindergartner was to help the child discover relationships in her plays and in all her experiences and to find meaning for herself.

Froebel was very much aware of the harmony possible between child development and the curriculum. He believed in child development in depth – body, mind, heart and soul – in harmony with God, humankind and nature. He referred to the senses as the doors to the inner child and believed that there should be a deepening of each sensory experience into the child's inner being.

Froebel's curriculum was a balanced curriculum. It began with an understanding of the Creator and continued with a knowledge of the creation, both the natural world as well as studies of mankind. Froebel considered his curriculum to be broad and referred to it as "all-sided". Educators may not know what potential lies dormant in a child. Therefore, it is very necessary to offer a broad curriculum.

If educators are to promote child development, they must possess not only a knowledge of child study but be confident that the various parts of the curriculum will further child development. A researcher studying child development should know the curriculum and the curriculum planner should be aware of the research into child study and the findings of that research. Educators need to discover what the child knows, what she needs to know in the present and what she might learn in the future. The kindergartner must also remember that the child is maturing and that the program is becoming correspondingly more complex. Therefore, she must plan always for the two to merge together at the child's *growing edge.* Froebel believed the two came together quite naturally through the child's play.

To re-discover Froebel's vision for kindergarten education is to become aware that each child in the kindergarten has the opportunity to be fully developed in an all-rounded way. Each child needs what all young people are seeking today, and which we must not deny them, *a fullness of experience.* This is possible, as Froebel suggested, through an in-depth development of each child growing in an all-rounded, harmonious way in relation to God, humankind and nature.

Educators and parents can be justly thankful for the early pioneers who had the vision and wisdom to introduce the Froebelian kindergarten into the public schools of Ontario. These men and women paved the way for the growth and development of a remarkable plan for early childhood education. There are tremendous benefits to be gained from accepting once again the Froebelian view of unity as the metaphysical basis of the kindergarten and from using once again

Froebel's method of education, *guided play*.

CHAPTER X

THE TWENTY YEARS FROM 1967 TO 1987

Between the 1960's and 1987, there have been a number of documents published in Ontario which have influenced the kindergarten but they have not altered it to any significant degree. Confusion still exists over the meaning and use of play in the child's education. Furthermore, kindergarten education is eclectic; there is still no common philosophical base of child development and education.

Influential documents of this period began with the publication of *Living and Learning: The Report of the Provincial Committee on Aims and Objectives of Education in the Schools of Ontario*, in 1968. The Ministry of Education also issued a number of books and reports such as *The Formative Years* and *Education in the Primary and Junior Divisions* in 1975, and in 1985 *Shared Discovery*. As well, *The Report of the Early Primary Education Project*, which grew out of a study on kindergarten and primary education, was released in 1985.

An extensive study was undertaken and supported by the Association des enseignants francoontariens, The Federation of Women Teachers' Associations of Ontario, Ontario English Catholic Teachers' Association and the Ontario Public School Men Teachers' Federation entitled *To Herald a Child: The Report of the Commission of Inquiry into the Education of the Young*

Child. More recently the F.W.T.A.O., Early Childhood Committee have issued a book entitled *Play, Active Learning in the Early School Years*.[1]

How can we best sum up the significant ideas which will take the kindergarten and early childhood education into the twenty-first century? Some of the views have been in the forefront of educational thinking for many years. We need now to assess and evaluate the worth of each idea. Those which are invalid we must discard. Those which are valid we must plan for and work towards their implementation.

A Unified Educational System From Kindergarten through College and University

Froebel had a vision for education which gave each child and young person the right to be educated through his or her own development. Froebel's plan for the process of education included, along with the thirst for knowledge, self-discipline and character development as well as the freedom to be creative. His was a long-range goal of developing mature young people who were not only well-educated but also responsible and compassionate human beings. He wrote:

Knowledge and application, consciousness and realization in

---

[1]All of these books are referred to later in this chapter. The footnotes are given where the references occur.

life united in the service of a faithful, pure, holy life, constitute the wisdom of life, pure wisdom. To be wise is the highest aim of man. . . .[2]

Such a vision cannot be accomplished in a year or even within a few years. It needs the encompassing support of all the educational institutions together working with the family.

Egerton Ryerson, Superintendent of Schools in Ontario from 1844 to 1876, and George Ross, Minister of Education from 1883 to 1899, both envisioned the Ontario public school system as an integrated whole. James Hughes saw the kindergarten as the foundation of that system. In 1968, *Living and Learning* referred to the possibility of an integrated education system from kindergarten to Grade Twelve. Over the past century there is no doubt that there have been those educators who have been very aware of the value of a unified system. It remains for us to see that that vision *does* become a reality.

Early Childhood Education, A Developmental Unit

The kindergarten was introduced into Ontario schools amid opposition, misunderstanding and criticism. Some felt the taxpayer should not be required to pay for children to play in a kindergarten. They felt children of that age should be home

with the mother. Others opposed an educational concept which seemed to ignore what they considered the real purpose of the school, the learning of the three R's. Many had no grasp of Froebel's creative play method, that it was through guided play the child understood not only the three R's but how to use them in meaningful ways. At the same time the child was developing lifelong attitudes and habits towards learning and work. As a result of negative criticisms, the kindergarten was limited to a one year experience and there it remained until the 1940's when the junior kindergarten was introduced adding a second year.

Certainly, there were early attempts to unify the child's early educational experience. During the first half of the twentieth century, kindergarten-primary classes were organized to combine kindergarten and primary education as well as to extend the idea of play and concrete learning up into the primary grades and eventually into the school grades. The door was opened to this progressive development but what in fact happened was that the three R's quickly moved down into the kindergarten. Certainly, the three R's were more easily understood as the business of the school and, therefore, mistakenly accepted as an appropriate early learning experience.

During the 1930's, in Toronto where many kindergartens had already been established, few kindergarten-primary classes were introduced. At the time, Emma Duff, a Toronto kindergartner, recommended that these early years from ages four to seven (kindergarten, kindergarten-primary,

---

[2]Friedrich Froebel, *The Education of Man*, p. 4.

and the first two grades) be a unit of education called the Childhood Department. The idea was well received but unfortunately nothing was done.

By 1939, the Primary Specialists Course was introduced into the Toronto Normal School and an attempt was made to draw together the kindergarten with the first two primary grades. This course was later extended downwards to include the theory and practice of junior kindergartens. In 1944, the Departmental Program of Studies presented these early years as an integrated whole. However, the battle was not won. For most people the kindergarten experience before grade one remained an optional one-year pre-school experience for a child.

Junior kindergartens introduced during the 1940's in Ottawa and Toronto did add a second year to the kindergarten experience. Since the 1960's other school boards in Ontario have also opened junior kindergartens. The extension of the kindergarten to include four-year-olds was a welcome advance but it did not resolve the need to give the child a unified early educational experience. These early years can be fractured when experiences for the young child are in nursery schools, daycares, junior and senior kindergartens and in the first two primary grades. For the sake of each child these years should be an integrated unit of education which allows the child to build an educational foundation.

As a first step towards uniting the first years of education, the writers of *Living and Learning* expressed the hope that all pre-school education would become the responsibility of the Department of Education in co-operation with school boards. Their Recommendation 115 stated that the Department of Education should;

> Assume the financing of nursery schools presently in operation, excluding private nursery schools, until the complete assimilation of nursery school education into the total education sequence can be accomplished.[3]

The *Report of the Early Primary Education Project* published in May of 1985 takes the issue much further. In fact, in the study sessions of the Committee they proposed the establishment of an integrated early childhood education unit.

> This unit, which now comprises JK to Grade 3 [ages 3+ to 8] would be ungraded; be flexible in terms of entry, attendance, and – for the younger children – length of day; and offer a range of programs and services through diversity in staffing.[4]

---

[3]Ontario, Department of Education, *Living and Learning, The Report of the Provincial Committee on Aims and Objectives in the Schools of Ontario*, Toronto: The Newton Publishing Co., 1968, p. 190.

[4]Ontario, Ministry of Education, *Report of the Early Primary Education Project* (May 1985), p. 15.

Such a proposal was part of their mandate along with recommending the introduction of junior kindergartens across the province.

In regard to curriculum, the central recommendations are that junior kindergarten (JK) be phased in throughout Ontario, and that the five years of the Primary Division (JK-Grade 3) be organized as an integrated unit. This unit would be characterized by continuity in both planning and program development, flexibility in pupil entry and progression, close attention to individual learning styles and developmental stages, and strong communication links with parents and others concerned with the education and well-being of young children. Consistent with its emphasis on an individualized approach, the Project recommends that "child learning profiles" be developed to identify the talents, interests, and needs of each pupil and suggest specific program adaptations.[5]

Certainly, the proposal in the Committee Report to integrate the early childhood years of education follow in Ontario's Froebelian tradition. Froebel saw the kindergarten years, the years from three to seven, as the foundation years of the educational system. Each child was to be developed as an individual within the context of all his relationships and he was to be educated *through his own development.*

The Kindergarten Unit: A Bridge Between the Home and School

Another aspect of the child's early years being one unit is the bridge the kindergarten provides between the home and the school. The concept of the kindergarten linking the home and school has been our heritage since the time of James Hughes who referred to it as the bridge which harmonized the two. In his day, however, the kindergarten idea was misunderstood; the one-year kindergarten for four and five-year-olds was considered by many as an expensive fad and certainly the idea of play as a means of learning was dismissed by most.

It is good for parents to be familiar with the educational principles of child development through parent evenings, courses and visits in the kindergarten. In such ways they become involved in their child's educational experience. The early kindergartners taught the children in the mornings and visited homes in the afternoons. Mothers' meetings and parent meetings were organized to help parents gain insights into Froebel's educational principles. The Institute of Child Study, University of Toronto has always encouraged parents to participate in their program and be involved in the studies with the children. Schools provide visiting days as well as special interview times. Kindergarten teachers also send home newsletters, plan activities or special

---

[5]*Ibid.,* p. i.

functions and include parents in field trips which keep them informed about the program.

The kindergarten is similar to a good home. Children are active and playful, the atmosphere is loving and caring and a special environment is provided for children. There is a caring and concern developed by the children for the others in the group and a respect for one another.

If the kindergarten can be organized into a team teaching arrangement with ungraded family groupings of children ages three to seven, it will also resemble the sibling relationships found in the family. Kindergarten is likely the first educational step outside the family for the young child and it is enough that he learn to co-operate with peers in a small group of children where he learns to share the adult. Gradually, the young child will learn to adjust to a larger group than can be experienced in the home, but during the kindergarten years, if it truly is to be the bridge, a child should not be required to fit initially into a group of 30 children. (infra, pp. 113-14).

The Kindergarten: The Foundation Years of the School System

That the foundation of the educational structure be laid during the child's early years is one of Froebel's purposes for the kindergarten. However, from the beginning the kindergarten with its method of play and learning through concrete

experience seemed to be something quite apart from the school with its emphasis on work and abstract learning.

If the kindergarten concept of education is truly to become the foundation of the education system, *it is the school that needs to be changed.* It is the school which must be transformed into a child development institution where students themselves are actively involved in the learning process and the staff, fulfilling their professional role as educators, guides that process. Generally speaking, this is not what has been happening. Instead there has been and still is considerable pressure for the kindergarten to be turned into a pre-school situation with a heavy emphasis on the three R's, the assumption being that an early academic start is the best way to prepare children for the school instructional program. School pressure has been exerted on the kindergarten to abandon its experiential approach towards child development and its emphasis on such invisible and fragile qualities as creativity, positive attitudes, self-activity and play.[6]

James Hughes had talked of *engrafting* the kindergarten onto the public school system. He expressed the need to think holistically, that

---

[6]It has been the author's experience that students who have the benefit of a Froebelian kindergarten foundation and all that it means in play and experience also have the potential to do better academically than youngsters who are "turned off" too early by a heavy-handed emphasis on the three R's.

educators see the kindergarten as the foundation of the educational structure. However, Froebel's kindergarten at that time presented a child development approach to education, whereas children attending Ontario schools were being instructed in subject matter. Froebel's method of education was play, while the school's approach was work, and often that work was seen as hard or even unpleasant. There were also those who believed that if education was not difficult as well as unpleasant, students could not possibly be learning. How could the Froebel kindergarten become the foundation of such a system?

The true kindergartner was not a teacher who instructed children but a *child nurturer, who developed and guided* the children. The idea that education, even difficult concepts, could or should be interesting and challenging to children, and that personal effort by the student to learn can bring joy are views that are still open to misunderstanding.

As early as the 1880's Leontine Newcomb of Hamilton spoke of a three or four-year kindergarten foundation to undergird the school system (*supra*, p. 56).

By the influence of the schools a nation has power to determine her own destiny. True citizenship as well as intellectual development is the keystone to the "national arch", and public education must cement the structures.
The foundation must be laid with the youngest as well as with the oldest child in our Schools, and the Froebelian Kindergarten, while completely adapted to the first three or four years of the child's schooling, must reach out through all the later periods of his education as the fundamental principle of all life growth and development.

In 1968, *Living and Learning*, expressed the need for the school to change in order that educators might build on the kindergarten foundation.

The traditional school was largely concerned with what the teacher taught and how effective he was in conducting an orderly class. The modern school is more concerned with what the pupils learn, why and how they learn and whether they will continue to be disposed to learn. All of this, and much more, is part of the school curriculum.[7]

If the kindergarten is to become the foundation of our education system, the school, too, must value the same aims and qualities, creative thinking and individual learning styles. Furthermore, students in the school grades must be challenged and encouraged to learn through their own efforts and experiences. There is no doubt that in following a child's best course of development that he can be educated in an all-rounded way and, therefore, live a fulfilling life.

---

[7]Ontario, Department of Education, *Living and Learning*, p. 123.

Child Development and the Curriculum

According to Froebel the curriculum needs to be both broad and thorough in order to develop the all-round child. In his organization of content Froebel suggested a triune framework which dealt with studies of *humankind, nature and God.* It was both broad and balanced, yet because he emphasized the child's experience, the child learned things within context. Guided by the kindergartner, the child learned the facts involved, became aware of their implications and found meaning for himself both of the facts and their many faceted relationships. Truly, the knowledge of relationships is what gives life and vitality to curriculum studies.

The document *Living and Learning* also divided curriculum studies into the three major areas; communications (the study of people), environmental studies (science and nature) and the humanities (a reflection on the ideas and values, philosophies and religions that shape our lives). In the Ministry document *Education in the Primary and Junior Divisions,* the curriculum is divided into communications, environmental studies and the arts, as part of the humanities. Values, goals and objectives are always included in these documents as a necessary part of the learning process. They take on meaning for the child as beliefs are internalized.

Teachers must not impose their own views on the children. The role of the teacher is to provide the context in which a child can develop values that reflect the priorities of a concerned society and at the same time recognize his or her integrity as an individual.[8]

The thrust of curriculum studies is the nurture and development of the whole child. The more the content can actually be experienced by the child because he is actively involved in the learning process, the broader will be the base of impressions he forms. Impressions are gathered, little by little, one at a time, each growing out of another, weaving together a network within the child which, in turn, provides a realistic and vital foundation for all his subsequent learning. The active child plays but he is also an *active* listener, an *active* reader, an *active* observer, and so on. A healthy young child becomes involved naturally because he is so full of energy. *Active* needs to be seen in contrast to *passive.* Is it not contradictory to speak of a *passive learner*?

That the child be at the centre of the Ontario school system is the message conveyed by the Ministry document, *Education in the Primary and Junior Divisions.* Child development is of prime importance.

Paramount to all curriculum decisions are the children and their individual ways of learning.

---

[8]Ontario, Ministry of Education, *Education in the Primary and Junior Division*, p. 20.

Observations gained by working alongside the child in an atmosphere of mutual trust will soon reveal both needs and interests to the teacher. This awareness of what each child needs, of how he or she learns, and of the extent to which he or she can be expected to generalize forms the basis of successful planning.

Teachers must SHOW that they care.[9]

The Grade System vs. Ungraded Family Groupings

Such a child development educational system calls for "the abolition of the graded system throughout the school; and the use of individual timetables at the senior level".[10] So states *Living and Learning.* In place of the grade system, that Committee advocated a learning continuum from kindergarten through grade twelve in which formal examinations would be abolished, except in necessary situations, and the evaluation of a student's progress would be ongoing by the classroom teacher.

Such a system of evaluation is based on trust in the classroom teacher. He or she is the professional who is depended upon to make an accurate assessment of each student's progress.[11] The teacher would compile a learning profile for each student. It would include information such as the child's learning style, daily accomplishments, group participation, attitudes, classroom tests, parent interviews, staff assessments, results of standardized testing and the like. The profile would also reveal the on-going and ever changing development of the child or student.

Individual charting of each student's progress is necessary in an ungraded system. The organization of the rooms would also need to be changed in order to provide for ungraded family groupings where education is thought of in units based on recognized stages of child development. At the Froebel Foundation, children ages three to seven are in the kindergarten which is the foundation of the educational structure. The school begins for the child at age eight and extends to our eldest group of students who are ages thirteen or fourteen. Children remain with their peer groups in an ungraded system and the content is adapted to the individuals. The task of the kindergartner is to see that each child progresses at his own level and is challenged at his growing edge in all areas of his development.

Can such a system become a reality in Ontario public schools? It is highly unlikely that any teacher, no

---

[9]*Ibid.*, p. 9.

[10]Ontario, Ministry of Education, *Living and Learning,* p. 76.

[11]Trust in the teacher implies a confidence in the teacher education programs as well as the ongoing professional development of that teacher (*infra*, pp. 142-43).

matter how skilled and proficient he or she is, can guide each child sufficiently well to develop all the potential that is there when there are over 30 children in the classroom. The more children for *U* whom a teacher is responsible, the less depth development will likely take place within each child. The ideal teaching/learning situation, of course, is the home, where there is already a family grouping, so that one child learns from other siblings as well as from the parents.

Group Size

Dr. Otto Weininger, Professor at the Ontario Institute for Studies in Education, referred to the negative effects on a child if the group becomes too large. In an article which appeared in a Newsletter of the Ontario Federation of Women Teachers, he was asked what research revealed about the effect of large classes on young children. He referred to a study of four-year-olds in which it was found that contacts with the children increased as the pupil-teacher ratio decreased. He also commented that young children lost a sense of self when they were part of too large a group, that group size being over 20 children.[12]

It is the policy of the Federation of Women Teachers' Associations of Ontario that no elementary class should exceed 15 students in number at the junior kindergarten level, 18 students in number at the senior kindergarten level, 20 students in number at the primary level and 25 students in number at the junior and intermediate levels, and that special consideration be given to factors such as physical and learning disabilities, socio-economic status, language, age of students, cultural background and environmental conditions.[13] While this policy has been recommended it has not yet been implemented.

The authors of the report, *To Herald A Child*, drew attention to the drawbacks of the high ratios of children to adult. They found that large classes did work against child development.

> While it is easy to talk about individualizing instruction, it is almost impossible to achieve on account of the overly large classes that exist in many schools.
> Even though there is controversy over the ideal class size, there is no doubt in teachers' minds that large classes affect the child adversely.[14]

[12]M. Howarth, "How Many Are Too Many? An Interview with Otto Weininger", *F.W.T.A.O. Newsletter* (February/March 1987), pp. 1-4.

[13]Early Childhood Committee, *Play, Active Learning in the Early School Years,* F.W.T.A.O., 1986, p. 39.

[14]Association des enseignants franco-ontariens, Federation of Women Teachers' Associations of Ontario, Ontario English Catholic Teachers' Association, Ontario Public School Men Teachers' Federation, *To Herald A Child*, The Report of the Commission of Inquiry into the Education of the Young Child, Toronto, p. 27.

At the Froebel Foundation the adult/child ratio is one to nine three, four and five-year-olds and one to twelve six and seven-year-olds. The various age groups come together in a larger group for circles and certain play activities. Where a child has a learning difficulty and attends the Froebel Foundation, he is placed in a small family grouping of children and, as well, receives daily one-to-one assistance.

Is Child Development Permissive or Progressive Education?

A distinction needs to be drawn between a permissive education and a progressive one. Progressive was a term given those educators who helped shape the New Education Movement at the turn of the last century. It referred to educators who placed the child in the centre of the educational process. Permissive is a fairly free and open style of education in which the child is given wide choices from an early age.

Exponents of permissive education have tended to join with the Progressivists because of the emphasis on child development and such Froebelian slogans as *follow the child.* To the Froebelian the words do not mean to follow the child in all his whims and fancies, but do mean to follow his developmental course and, therefore, to guide him into the most appropriate activities. In progressive education the child is guided into those activities which are best for him and he is challenged to put forth his best efforts. Permissiveness, however, is indulgence. It is to sound education what self-indulgence is to physical

fitness and can only weaken and spoil what would otherwise be a healthy, wholesome education.

Permissive educators tend to believe that everything a child chooses is good, while Progressive educators view the child as having the potential for both goodness and badness. Progressives acknowledge that the child needs guidance by a caring adult in order to bring out the good and prevent bad qualities from growing.

Froebel, as a progressive educator, would have the child begin life within the context of God's love and always develop and grow in harmony with him. Thus, the child's conscience is developed, rooted in a tender heart. The child learns self-discipline as he understands and lives out God's principles in his life. His will is strengthened from within himself to perform *the good and true* throughout his life.

Jesus took a little child and put him in the midst of the adults, saying, "Except ye. . . become as little children, you shall not enter into the kingdom of heaven."[15] Young children are trusting of others, unsophisticated and true to their inner selves. However, they do have the potential for wrongdoing. They certainly make mistakes because of their lack of knowledge and experience of life. A young child doesn't even foresee the consequences of his own actions. Yet, a child

---

[15]Matthew 18:3, the *Bible*, King James Version.

growing truly in the love of God will learn how to choose the good and refuse the wrong. A child who is respected and encouraged in such a positive manner will learn to act in a positive way. That is the emphasis in a progressive education.

Progressive education also views the child within the context of relationships. Individual child development takes place within certain settings – the family, the church, educational institutions and so on – and means that a child's unique abilities, skills and interests are being developed within those relationships. A child growing in relationship to all about him has the opportunity of becoming a caring, self-disciplined, dependable human being. He is becoming aware of his own person, yet he is discovering, given his unique potential, how to interact with others and with his environment. As he matures, he becomes aware that one day he will be ready to fulfill his destiny, his purpose in life, as an educated, responsible and compassionate human being. This growing awareness of relationships helps him to bring his life into balance and perspective.

Progressive educators place the child in the centre of the education system to help him become a well-rounded, responsible person. Permissive educators also place the child in the centre but by indulging him there is always the danger he will become self-centred and selfish.

The Method of Kindergarten Education: Play

The most productive method of educating the young child, ages three to seven, is through his own energy. Because that energy is expressed in activity the child is to be educated through his own play.

Play, which has several faces, allows for a continual flow of child development. The playing child learns about his world as he plays with concrete objects and materials and they provide him with the materials for creative expression. Play is a complete activity; the child forms impressions through his senses, which are the doors to the inner child, as he interacts with other children and the kindergartner. His experiences become clear and accurate to him as he is guided by the kindergartner who wisely uses both word and song to complement his activity. His interest in things causes him to become involved, to repeat favourite activities or to explore new avenues and, as well, he harmonizes the new learning with the old.

The playing child is motivated by his own ideas and guided in his plans and actions by the kindergartner. As he shares his play with others, he develops skills of large and fine muscle coordination, understanding and attitudes of self-discipline such as self-control and patience, and qualities such as kindness and thoughtfulness. He is willing to put forth effort to accomplish his plan. His attention span is growing and he is experiencing what it is to persist and to develop endurance. The young child is beginning an educational experience which will lead him to accomplish worthwhile goals throughout his life, given his particular energies and abilities, and because he is playing, all is accomplished in the spirit of happiness and joy.

The Ministry document, *Education in the Primary and Junior Divisions*, stressed the importance of the child's play.

Play is an essential part of learning. It is free from the restrictions of reality, external evaluations, and judgement. Children can try out different styles of action and communication without being required to make premature decisions or being penalized for errors. Play provides a context in which the teacher can observe children's handling of materials and social situations, assess their stage of development, and encourage experiences that further their growth. The teacher should know when to intervene unobtrusively, when to add to or change a play situation, when to provide a toy telephone, a costume, a question, or a suggestion that will further the fantasy or broaden the experience.[16]

In February of 1986 the Federation of Women Teachers' Associations of Ontario issued a publication entitled *Play, Active Learning in the Early School Years*. In it, the Early Childhood Education Committee stated the F.W.T.A.O.'s support of *play* as the means of learning for young children.

It is the policy of the Federation of Women Teachers' Association of Ontario that a curriculum designed around play provides young children in school with the opportunity to achieve optimal development in an active learning environment.[17]

Why is it, then, when there is such official support of play as the method of education for young children, that it is not more widely accepted and used by teachers?

In the report, *To Herald A Child* the right of the young child to express himself in play and to learn through play was recognized. The Commission felt teachers should make clear "that through play the child has learned about his world and also to question, to wonder, to explore, to imagine, to predict and to experience himself and others". However, the Commission did not always find *the practice of play* in early childhood education settings. The Commission report went so far as to say that the absence of play along with the present emphasis on a grade system made "a mockery of child-oriented education".

---

[16]Ontario, Ministry of Education, *Education in the Primary and Junior Divisions*, pp. 15-16.

[17]*FWTAO Guidebook*, 1985, p. 236, cited in Early Childhood Committee, *Play, Active Learning in the Early School Years*,, F.W.T.A.O., 1986, p. 7.

To some, play was considered part of leisure-time and totally unrelated to work, while for others play was considered a reward for work well done. [18] It is obvious that more effort needs to be made to help all teachers understand *play* as *the method of education.*

There certainly is this need to clarify what play truly is and can be to a child in his development and education. At its deepest level play is also the working out by the child of inner thoughts, ideas and feelings. He needs to learn to listen to his inner being and to tap the resources within himself. Play is his creative expression. All children *are creative;* it remains for us as parents and educators to draw out that creativity. Further, the playful *attitude* is positive, open and flexible and the child develops an ever broadening awareness.

Children have a right to expect a teacher to help them keep in touch with their inner selves; with their thoughts, feelings and creative expressions. A wise teacher or kindergartner observes his or her children and listens to them in order that each child might be understood and developed in a way that is true to the child's own and full potential. As Froebel wrote over eighty years ago, "The spontaneous play of the child discloses the future inner life of the man."[19]

---

[18]Commission of Inquiry, *To Herald a Child,* p. 25, 29.

[19]Froebel, *Education of Man,* p. 55.

Self-Discipline: the transformation of play energy into work energy

Play and work are expressions of energy and one can be transformed into the other as the child matures. The process is one of self-discipline. Energy flows from the young child. He enjoys play for its own sake; he may or may not have an end result in view, and stops only when he is tired. The boy in the eight to eleven stage is beginning to want to see some worthwhile results from his efforts, so he willingly practices the principles of self-discipline in order to achieve his goal. It is important that his efforts be encouraged by adults in order for him to maintain a positive attitude. It is only as the child makes a commitment of the will to do his best that he will do so. The willingness to put one's best effort into a task provides strong motivation to persist. Thus, a child will begin to develop endurance and patience, continuing until the task is done or the difficulty overcome. It is then that he experiences the joy of accomplishment.

Habits of consistency and effort were to be developed in each child. Froebel suggested that a child of six or seven years have work tasks to perform for about an hour each day. The tasks should be suited to the child's maturity and level of development. He warned parents not to discourage a youngster from helping them. Young children may be of little help but they do like to try. In their play they often imitate adults at work. After very few refusals of "Don't bother me now" or "I haven't time to let you help," the young child feels he is of no real use and develops *that negative attitude* of thought. As a result, when he is eight or nine years old and really could be helpful he no longer offers.

Parents and educators should avoid fostering negative attitutes in children. A young child shut out of the real work of the family, the child who is indulged or the child who is neglected will not likely develop positive attitudes towards work. Sometimes a child does not understand a task or how to do it and the work becomes too hard in a way it should not. Perhaps the work is hard because it requires patience, endurance and persistence and the child may give in too easily. Also, it is very unwise to superimpose adult views on a child's activity by calling art, toys and games *play* while activities relating to printing, reading and mathematics are called *work*. A young child makes no such distinctions in his activity.

How important it is to help the child become self-disciplined in the use of his own energy! Through his play activities and specific work tasks, it is possible gradually to lengthen the time a task takes as well as to add further jobs. The young person needs to be educated to harness his energies for good and useful purposes.

Cultivating in the child a positive attitude towards effort and helping him develop skills of self-discipline are important to the growing, developing child. He needs to develop skills in organizing and planning his time, making the best use of his energies and learning to use resources wisely. Habits cultivated when he is young are long lasting and difficult to change at a later time.

As play is an expression of inner creative self-activity, work, too, can be creative for the adult. The issue is not whether play is the forerunner of work or whether it is not, but rather how to help educators and parents understand the potential of child play which becomes the adult's work. Thus, over a period of time, as the child matures and develops into a self-disciplined person, the same energy formerly used in play is *transformed* into work energy.

A child who plays thoroughly, with self-active determination, persevering until physical fatigue forbids will surely be a thorough, determined man, capable of self-sacrifice for the promotion of the welfare of himself and others.[20]

The Kindergartner's Role

A kindergartner, a child nurturer, is a member of a team which works with young children ages three to seven in a family grouping arrangement. Each kindergartner on the team shares responsiblity for the large group while at the same time having a particular concern for a smaller group of the children. The purpose of the kindergartners over the four- or five-year kindergarten span is to help each one of the children develop fully in an

---

[20]*Ibid.*, p. 55.

all-rounded way and as well, to lay an educational foundation in impressions and attitudes by means of personal experience.

The kindergartner is to develop each child in the context of all his relationships beginning with the group of children. She also heeds the child's affinity with the natural environment. In the playyard, on neighbourhood walks and travelling from home to kindergarten, the child soon becomes aware of the names of trees, flowers and all living things. Thus, a respect and caring can be cultivated for all of God's creation. There is also a sense of God's love demonstrated by the care given to the child as well as gained by listening to stories of Jesus and his compassion for others. Young children possess a feeling for relationship, a sense of the unity in their world. Unfortunately, as they mature, education can cause this initial sense of wholeness to be fractured and fragmented. The cause of such fracturing may be partly due to the failure of the child's educators to guide him into the relatedness of experiences one with one another and to himself.

How can a kindergartner hope to develop each child fully and, at the same time, make him aware of the interrelatedness of things? Certainly to do so, kindergartners need to understand and utilize basic principles of education. For example:

1. Foundations are laid in the family during the early childhood years. The context of life is the love and respect shared one with another.

Froebel called the family *the sanctuary of humanity.*

2. The law of life to which Froebel referred is a process of growth and development found in all of the natural creation. There are no easy solutions; there is no magic wand. Growth takes time, the potential is in the seed and development is a process.

3. The method of education during the early years is play. The play method is doublesided, for the child both learns about the world in which he lives and develops skills from within. Play energy is the root of work energy. Through play a child exercises *transforming power,* developing imagination and creativity.

4. Curriculum content, because it nourishes the child, needs to be balanced and wholesome. It should also be broad and visionary and, at the same time, thorough and exact. Children internalize course content by means of experience.

5. The Froebel Gifts and Art Occupations, toys and materials with which the children play, help them to become both creative and self-active. A child learns by doing and should be encouraged to talk about his activity.

6 If educators instruct, if words run ahead of the child's experience, all is lost, and his education becomes hollow, dead and mechanical. The kindergartner or the teacher must

keep pace with the child and guide the learning processes going on within him.

7. Self-discipline brings all into harmony. The child is *becoming;* too little is insufficient and too much spoils. Each person must learn to exercise the effort to overcome difficulties, to order resources and time so that he might fulfill his destiny as a creative person contributing to the welfare of others.[21]

A great deal then, is expected of the children's guide. The educator plans with the children, makes choices concerning the learning environment and is expected to interpret and evaluate the program *with* and *for* each child. Such an expectation, as the writers of *Living and Learning* so wisely noted, makes considerably more demands upon a teacher than the traditional method of instruction where students sat in rows at their desks waiting to be told what assignment to do.

The modern curriculum is concerned more with the learning experience of the pupil than with the instructional performance of the teacher. It asks the teacher to select, organize, and guide learning experiences which meet the needs of the child, and to do this effectively by application of sound principles of learning.

Clearly, this shift of emphasis away from instruction demands more, not less, from the teacher.[22]

A statement taken from *Shared Discovery*, a Ministry Document published in 1985, gives some indication of the Ministry's expectations for teachers:

Planning involves setting program objectives based on interpretations of observations of the child and a knowledge of developmental growth (growth strands) and of how learning takes place. In planning an individualized program, the teacher will have to answer the following question: "What knowledge, cognitive - skill, affective - development, and psychomotor - skill objectives should I set for the child?" The teacher should also involve the child in the planning of his/her learning activities.

At times during the observation of a child the teacher may be able to plan appropriate learning opportunities that will immediately extend the child's learning. In other cases, the teacher may require time to develop further plans. In either case, the learning decided on should be integrated into the

---

[21]For a further development of these principles see Barbara Corbett, *A Garden of Children*, The Froebel Foundation, 1980.

[22]Ontario, Department of Education, *Living and Learning*, p. 75.

day-to-day experiences of the child.[23]

While the environment and the child's activity within that environment are essential ingredients of learning through play, it is the quality of the interaction between the kindergartner and the child which turns the child's activity into education.[24] She interacts with the child in a variety of ways; by her responses in words or the smiles and frowns of body language, through her use of stories, poems, songs and games, her choice of activities and experiences, and certainly by her suggestions and encouragement. She remains neither aloof from the child's play nor does she allow him to wander aimlessly. Yet, she does not interfere with his play because that would weaken his powers of action. She protects him from danger but she gives him freedom to explore, to discover and to make mistakes. The child feels free to be himself.

In our modern educational system expectations for teachers of young children are high and demanding but also unrealistic where classes are large. Teachers are involved throughout the school day with the children and must find time before the children come or after they leave to carry out all the planning and preparation necessary. Yet, there is also the suggestion that teachers be involved in drawing up local programs of study to fit in with the Ministry guidelines.

The policy of the Ministry of Education has been to provide Boards of Education with guidelines and broad goals. In the booklet, *The Formative Years*, the Ministry has suggested that local staff and teachers be involved in the specific program planning for their areas.

> . . . it is the responsibility of the local school boards - through their supervisory officials - to formulate local programs that are within the rationale of the provincial policy and at the same time, reflect local needs and priorities.[25]

Teachers need to be actively involved in program planning in some capacity for they are the ones who implement the programs with the children. Each has a valuable contribution to make out of his/her own experience and reflection, important in program planning. But where do treachers find the time for such work during the teaching year? One idea might be to hire these teachers for the summer months to work on program content.

Michael Fullan and F. Michael Connelly who, in 1987, completed a

---

[23]Ontario, Ministry of Education, *Shared Discovery; Teaching and Learning in the Primary Years*, 1985, p. 15.

[24]For an explanation of Froebel's guided play see Barbara E. Corbett, *A Garden of Children*, Chapters VIII and XI.

[25]Ontario, Ministry of Education, *The Formative Years*, 1975, p. 2.

position paper for the Ministry of Colleges and Universities on teacher education in Ontario have been critical of the actual participation teachers have in curriculum planning.[26] They found the present system of curriculum writing too removed from the average classroom teacher.

> Teachers were, of course, involved, but it is a very different thing to have a centralized board authority call the shots and invite local, hand-picked teachers into the inner sanctum of curriculum planning than it is to put the responsibility for teachability in the hands of teachers themselves.[27]

Another area of concern which relates to the effectiveness of kindergartners is the availability of research information. More studies are needed which provide kindergartners with practical and helpful insights. It may not be necessary to do a great many more studies but rather to see that the results of those done are easily accessible to the classroom teacher. Results made readily available through professional development programs and publications could help research insights become common knowledge throughout the teaching profession.

The Ministry urges teachers to communicate with one another and to share their knowledge and experiences in order to benefit each child. Fullan and Connelly noted, "Good teachers working with other good teachers get even better."[28] The professional educator is both a scholar and a learner. He or she needs to continue studying, to read professional journals and to be active in professional organizations in order to grow by means of the stimulation and encouragement from others. However, the essential ingredient that kindergartners bring to the education profession, besides their own personalities, is the quality of teacher training they have received.

The Education of Kindergartners

Over the years ways of improving the standards of education have been suggested. For example, periodically, the idea of a province-wide testing program resurfaces as a solution for improving standards. Such a recommendation appeared in George Radwanski's report for the Ministry of Education, *Ontario Study of the Relevance of Education, and the Issue of Dropouts,*

> That standardized province-wide tests at least in reading comprehension, writing (including grammar, spelling and punctuation), mathematics, reasoning and problem-solving, and learning skills, as well as in

[26]Michael Fullan and F. Michael Connelly, *Teacher Education in Ontario: Current Practice and Options for the Future*, Position Paper, Toronto, Ontario; Ministry of Colleges and Universities, 1987.

[27]*Ibid.*, p. 54.

[28]*Ibid.*, p. 55.

other core curriculum subjects in high school, be administered to all elementary and high school students at appropriate intervals throughout the years of schooling.[29]

A province-wide testing system could seriously threaten teacher training as well as day to day education. The proposal establishes as a goal *success on tests* without acknowledging that tests have very limited use; they can only measure performance on a specific task. With such an emphasis the three R's, the tools of education, become ends in themselves and their reason for being is lost sight of. Such an emphasis on testing channels education into a utilitarian goal which, in turn, threatens to negate all the intangibles involved in developing and educating the well-rounded, thinking, creative person. Those qualities are the main thrust of education yet they are very difficult to measure. If we pursue the idea of province-wide testing, making success on written tests the sole yardstick for evaluation, what will happen to the necessary child development goal?

It is not that the three R's should be ignored, but it must always be remembered that they are tools. An excellent mastery of the tools of education combined with the development of the creative, responsible, young person is a worthwhile goal in education. The future of the education system does not rest in its testing program but it is to be realized in teacher education.

Education is both an art and a science. The study of children as well as the study of each child is a science, as is the study of curricula. However, the interaction and communication between the kindergartner and the children is not so easily analyzed and identified, for it is dependent on many intangibles and sensitivities. The dynamic of interaction is an art. Student kindergartners, then, need to learn the process of education as both an art and a science.

Reference has been made to the position paper on teacher education by Michael Fullan and F. Michael Connelly. The authors hope the paper will stimulate discussion of a new model of teacher education.[30] While they do not feel their views will be accepted as they now stand, they hope there will be an open form of fresh and creative thinking on the process of training professional educators.

> We use the term "reshaping" because we want to draw attention to our view that it is the overall countenance of teacher education, rather than any one of its parts, that needs reform.[31]

---

[29]George Radwanski, *Ontario Study of the Relevance of Education, and the Issue of Dropouts*, Toronto, Ontario, Ministry of Education, 1987, p. 199.

[30]Fullan and Connelly, *Teacher Education in Ontario . . .*, p. 7.

[31]*Ibid.*, p. 58.

There are many factors to consider in planning a kindergartner training course, especially now that teachers' colleges in Ontario have been phased out and all teacher training takes place at the university. Some of the factors relate to course content and the overall length of the program, while others are concerned with child study and practice teaching. Teacher education needs a thorough review to prepare the teachers of the future for the challenging task awaiting them. Obviously, such preparation, while it is the culmination of all the previous education the trainee has had, cannot be accomplished in one year, nor can it be done solely in the lecture rooms of our colleges and universities.[32]

The professional skill of the educator is to learn to draw out and develop human potential by means of curricula. Such an approach to education is much more demanding and challenging for kindergartners than merely teaching course content. We need an educational system that *develops* our children and young people and, as well, encourages each one in the skills and scholarship that match that inner potential.

Philosophy courses and methods courses are essential if educators are to understand the indissoluble link between theory and practice. Educational principles allow the student kindergartner flexibility and offer a basis for choice-making in working with the children. For example, one principle would be to view education as growth. The application of this principle varies with each child because each one grows at an individual rate. Recognizing and acknowledging that rate becomes relevant in the timing of presenting appropriate material to the child. Each principle, then, becomes a course of study in itself.

Other examples could be used to demonstrate the marriage between theory and practice. That the relationship be understood through practical experience is essential in the teaching and training of kindergartners. Otherwise students will be left with an eclectic view of education, without guidelines and, therefore, have no basis for choice-making.

The practice-teaching experience rounds out theoretical studies by giving the student kindergartner opportunities to relate ideas with practice. One suggestion is to place students with the same children on a long-term basis. First of all, they would begin to discover the developmental patterns in children by becoming involved right away in the responsibilities for which they are being prepared. Secondly, the consistent ongoing experience would help them understand children, individual learning styles and the way curriculum content is used to develop each child. Such a practice-teaching change could help place the emphasis on the child as a learner rather than leaving it where it has been, on the teaching of grade subjects to children.

[32]It is with constraint that any comments are made on teacher education. For a thorough discussion of the topic see the position paper by Fullan and Connelly.

The same goal worth striving for in teacher training is of value at all levels of education. The goal is the ongoing development of the self-active, creative person as a responsible and compassionate human being. One goal, relevant throughout the education system, would help educators focus on the educational process as a continuum. Student teachers should be encouraged to show initiative and responsibility in planning and working out their own ideas from basic guidelines. Teacher training institutions also need to provide ways and means of guiding their students to realize and utilize the self-active, creative potential within themselves, otherwise, how are they going to develop that potential in children? Then, too, they will, in turn, provide examples for the children they teach. Their own professional education must help them *to become* as well as *to achieve*. However, such development in student teachers will only occur as faculty members and experienced teachers, on an ongoing basis, act as *guides* and *mentors* for them.

In summary then, both student teachers and professional educators need the freedom, as well as encouragement and support, if they are to show initiative in working through the educational processes with children. Obviously, it is the children who will receive the benefit when educators find adventure and fulfillment in their profession, a profession which seeks to develop the potential in children by means of educational experience and outer awareness.

The Task Ahead

The time has come to clarify ideas and highlight priority goals in order to plan how to carry through the process of accomplishment. Some of the tasks in relation to Early Childhood Education to be undertaken are:

- Formal education should be viewed as a continuum, kindergarten through college or university, and an attempt made throughout the entire system beginning with teacher training to guide students according to sensible and wholesome educational principles.

- The first five years of education are to become an Early Childhood Education Unit which includes children from the junior kindergarten to the end of grade two. This foundation unit is to provide for each child's unique learning style and continuous progress.

- The Early Childhood Education Unit also needs to serve as a *bridge* between the home and school. It is important that this bridge be a family grouping of children from ages three or four to seven.

- For these early years to be the *foundation* of the school system, the school must change. It, too, must educate students *by means of* personal development and experiential learning, the process being both purposeful and flexible.

- If the curriculum is to nourish and develop each child, it must be both broad and wholesome. For the child to be developed by education, impressions must be gained through personal experience.

- The number of children in a group should be low enough to allow the kindergartner sufficient time and energy to listen to and interact with *each child* in a meaningful way.

- Progressive education, placing the child in the centre of the process, means that the potential within each child is developed in an all-round way. A child is to be neither indulged nor spoiled by an adult's permissive attitude.

- The young child is to be educated *through play. Play is the expression of energy* which shows a child to be both creative and self-active. The maturing young person in the school, growing in self-discipline, learns how to harness that energy for work tasks. Therefore, work becomes a disciplined, creative expression.

- The kindergartner is the child's *guide.* To educate by developing the child, the kindergartner limits choices in the educational environment to those which serve child development. There are ideas and skills to be experienced and understood by the child which, in turn, allow freedom for further creative expression and productive accomplishment.

- Teachers are a valuable resource in curriculum planning because they are the ones experiencing most directly the learning/teaching process. Appropriate time planning could free these *front-line* educators for research and curriculum design.

- The child, the teacher and the student teacher need both freedom and encouragement to be self-active and creative persons throughout the educational process. The role of the Ministry, school boards and teacher training institutions is to support that initiative.

- Teacher education needs to be reviewed and placed in a refreshing context of meaning if it is truly to prepare the educators of the future. At least a three year training experience at the university combining arts and science courses with education courses is more realistic in view of the task to be done.

By tracing the development of kindergarten education in Ontario, it becomes obvious that the theory is in place. For over 100 years educators in Ontario have advocated a progressive view of education, education by development, and provincial grants have been given for kindergarten education. Decision-makers and educators need now to work together in order to ensure that concise and effective decisions are taken to improve the education of young children. There are major decisions, and likely costly ones, ahead. Those decisions must be made with the first priority in place, and that is the children themselves.

APPENDIX

INTERVIEWS 1965 TO 1966

Kindergarten Teachers

NAME	LOCATION
Aedy, Edna	Fort William
Babel, Penny	Kirkland Lake
Bates, Eleanor	Sault Ste Marie
Black, Joan	Port Arthur
Bryan, Mary P.	Toronto Township
Carter, Isabell	Sarnia
Chapman, Maxine	Belleville
Chappell, M. S.	Southampton
Chisholm, E. J.	Goderich
Connolly, I.	Peterborough
Cory, Emily	Goderich
Dauphinee, Francis L.	Ottawa
Dunn, Helene M.	Sault Ste Marie
Fish, June E.	Halton No. 2
Freeman, Doris	Timmins
Harris, Katherine	London
Hauser, N.	Kingston
Holmes, Margaret	London
Lidstone, Doris	Bracebridge
Lowe, Irene	Muskoka No 3
McArthur, Louise	Port Arthur
MacEachern, M.	Gravenhurst
McKillop, Ruth	Ottawa
Macpherson, Iris	St. Catharines
Macquarrie, M.	Kirkland Lake
Malcolm, D. Enid	Belleville
Malone, Patricia	London
Malvern, Dorothy	Windsor
Matthie, Elaine	Brantford
Morris, Dorothy	Oakville
Myers, Dorothy	Cornwall
Nichols, Hilary	Oakville
Northrop, Jeanette	Peterborough
Parslow, Elizabeth J.	Fort William
Pearce, Jo-Ann	London
Preston, Esther	Kingston
Purcell, Anne	Kingston
Rathwell, Norma	Ottawa
Robinson, Nina	Timmins
Schotach, Bonnie	Toronto Township
Shaver, Frieda	London
Shaw, Barbara	Owen Sound
Sherwood, C.	Stratford
Smith, May J.	Stratford
Stinson, Irene	Ayton
Taylor, Shirley	Owen Sound
Webster, Marjorie	Windsor
Willis, Margaret	Port Arthur
Wilson, Jean	North Bay

Kindergarten-Primary Supervisors and Consultants

NAME	LOCATION
Bailey, Cora E.	Peterborough
Beatty, Phyllis	Belleville
Cross, Marion	St. Catharines
Gaston, Helen	Etobicoke
McKaig, M.	Sarnia
McLellan, Marjorie	London
Assistants	
Cornwall, Marion	
Drummond, Jean	
Dunbar, Norma	
Marsh, Betty	Hamilton
Morgan, Mary	Essex No. 5
Smith, Audrey	Windsor
Steeves, Thelma	Sandwich E
Walpole, Pearl	Toronto Tnsp (Mississauga)
Wetmore, Lorina J.	Ottawa
Wettlaufer, M.	Toronto

Municipal and Provincial Inspectors

NAME	INSPECTORATE
Municipalities	
Carson, K. O.	Halton No. 2
Cousins, J. M.	Belleville
Gray, A. E.	Fort William
Hunter, H. C.	Kingston
Judge, J. C.	Essex No. 5
Pace, J.	Sault Ste. Marie
Counties	
Clark, L. W.	Grey No. 2
Coulter, J. W.	Huron No. 2
Ellis, N. W.	Leeds No. 1
McClelland, J.	Ontario No. 4
MacInnes, W. S.	Bruce No. 1
Peat, J.R.M.	Welland No. 1, Haldimand No. 2
and	
	Lincoln No. 3
Rae, W. G.	Grey No. 3
Sturgeon, D.	
Taylor, Mary	Primary Education Area 4, Western Ontario
Thomas, R. F.	Gray No. 1 and City of Owen Sound
Waldie, T. K.	Bruce No. 3
Districts	
Gerow, W. J.	Thunder Bay No. 3
Hammell, W. F.	Muskoka No. 3
Lowcock, J. S.	Thunder Bay No. 2
McCluskie, L. E.	Nipissing No. 2 and City of North Bay
Tindall, A. E.	Cochrane No. 2, Algoma No. 2 and Sudbury No. 5

Retired Kindergartners

NAME	LOCATION
Adams, Eva	Peterborough
Baggs, Hazel	Toronto
Buxton, Lauretto	Hamilton
Dickson, Gladys	Toronto
Duckworth, Phillis	Windsor
Fisher, Alma	Hamilton
Fleming, Frances	Owen Sound
Haygarth, Fanny	Windsor
Hume, Esther	Goderich
Hunt, Margaret	Hamilton
Hutchinson, Augusta	London
Lyons, Mary	Brantford
McIntosh, Grace	Brantford
Murry, Evelyn	Toronto
Nicol, Mina	Owen Sound
Richardson, Ethel	Peterborough
Robinson, Phyllis	Hamilton
Scott, Alberta	Fort William
Slinn, Nan	Ottawa
St. John, Gertrude	Toronto
Webb, Hazel E.	Sault Ste. Marie

Other Persons

Directors of Education, Superintendents of Public Schools and Public School Principals have not been listed, but without their helpful co-operation the study could not have been undertaken. There were also a number of teachers in Southern Ontario and the Metropolitan Toronto area, besides those listed, who willingly expressed their opinions concerning the kindergarten.

- Mary Austin
  Kindergarten Teacher,Toronto
- Claire S. Burke
  Formerly Instructor,
  Primary Specialists'Course,Toronto
  Teacher's College
- Jean Care
  Kindergarten Teacher, Forest Hill
- Ruth Devry
  Kindergarten Teacher, Toronto
- Margaret Dryden
  Formerly Assistant, Toronto Normal
  School Kindergarten
- M. Evans
  Supervising Principal,Teck, T.S.A.
- D. C. Fuller
  Instructor, Primary Specialists'
  Course,Toronto Teachers' College
- Dorothea Graham
  Kindergarten Teacher,
  Formerly Kindergarten Assistant
  Ottawa Normal School
- N. Grant
  Supervising Principal, North Bay
- Chester Lunde
  Chicago
- Erling Lunde
  Chicago
- Laura Hughes Lunde
  Chicago
- Mary Macintyre
  Formerly Kindergarten Director, Toronto
  Normal School Kindergarten

- Dorothy A. Millichamp
  Associate Professor and Supervisor of
  Academic Program, Institute of Child
  Study, University of Toronto
- Dorothy Moncur
  Instructor, Institute of Child Study,
  University of Toronto
- P. A. Moore
  Instructor, Peterborough Teacher's College,
  Formerly Curriculum Branch, Ministry of
  Education
- Flora Morrison
  Instructor,Institute of Child Study
  University of Toronto
- R. Nixon
  Public Relations, Hamilton Board of
  Education
- Margaret Stevens
  Kindergarten Teacher, Peel
- P. L. Smye
  Instructor, Primary Specialists' Course,
  Hamilton Teacher College
- H. Stevenson
  Principal, Scarborough Public School
- S. Taylor
  Principal, Gravenhurst Public School
- W. Wylie,
  Supervising Principal, Dundas

SELECTED BIBLIOGRAPHY

Public Documents

Fullan, Michael; and Connelly, Michael. *Teacher Education in Ontario: Current Practice and Options for the Future.* Position paper. Toronto: Ministry of Colleges and Universities, 1987.

Hamilton. *Minutes of the Proceedings of the Board of Education.* 1889-1900, 1902-1904.

LaPierre, Laurier, Commissioner. *To Herald a Child, The Report of the Commission of Inquiry into the Education of the Young Child,* Toronto. 1980.

Hodgins, J. George. *Special Report on the Ontario Educational Exhibition. 1876.* Toronto: Hunter, Ross & Co., 1877.

LaPierre, Laurier, Commissioner. *To Herald a Child, The Report of the Commission of Inquiry into the Education of the Young Child,* Toronto. 1980.

London. *Annual Report, the Board of Education,* 1885-1964.

Morgan, S. A. *The Montessori Method: An Exposition and Criticism.* Ontario Department of Education, Bulletin No. 1. Toronto: L. K. Cameron, Printer, 1913.

Ontario, Department of Education. *Syllabus of Studies and Regulations for Kindergarten, 1908.* Toronto: L. K. Cameron, 1908.

Ontario, Department of Education. *Programme for Junior and Senior Kindergarten and Kindergarten Primary Classes of the Public and Separate Schools,* 1944.

Ontario, Department of Education. *Kindergarten.* 1966.

Ontario, Department of Education. *Circular 19* (in the Provincial Archives).

Ontario, Department of Education. *Interim Revision, Introduction and Guide.* 1967.

Ontario, Department of Education. *Living and Learning: The Report of the Provincial Committee on Aims and Objectives in the Schools of Ontario.* Toronto: The Newton Publishing Co., 1968.

Ontario Educational Association Proceedings. 1873-1966.

Ontario, Ministry of Education, *Education in the Primary and Junior Division.* 1975.

Ontario, Ministry of Education. *The Formative Years.* 1975.

Ontario, Ministry of Education. *Report of the Early Primary Education Project.* May 1985.

Ontario, Ministry of Education. *Shared Discovery: Teaching and*

Learning in the Primary Years.
1985.

Ontario. *Report of the Royal
Commission on Education.*
Toronto: Baptist Johnston, 1950.

Ontario. *Reports of the Minister of
Education.* 1882-1965.

Ontario. *Revised Statutes*, II. 1887.

Ottawa. *Minutes of the Proceedings
of the Public School Board.* 1888-
1964.

Radwanski, George. *Ontario Study of
the Relevance of Education and the
Issue of Dropouts*, Toronto,
Ontario: Ministry of Education,
1987.

Toronto. *Annual Report of the
Inspector of Public Schools.*
1883, 1888-1932.

Toronto. *Minutes of the Proceedings
of the Public School Board.* 1876-
1966.

Books

Althouse, J. G. "Centenary Address,"
*The Toronto Normal School,
1847-1947.* Toronto: School of
Graphic Arts, 1947.

The Bible, King James Version.

Blats, William E.; Millichamp,
Dorothy; and Fletcher, Margaret.
*Nursery Education, Theory and
Practice.* New York: William
Morrow and Co., 1935.

Blats, William E.; *Understanding The
Young Child.* Toronto: Clarke,
Irwin and Co. Ltd., 1944.

Blow, Susan E. *Educational Issues in
the Kindergarten.* New York:
D. Appleton and Co., 1909.

Corbett, Barbara E. *A Garden of
Children.* Mississauga: The
Froebel Foundation, 1980.

Curtis, S. J. *History of Education in
Great Britain.* London: University
Tutorial Press Ltd., 1961.

Dewey, John. *How We Think.*
Boston: D. C. Heath & Co., 1910.

--------. *Democracy and Education.*
New York: The Macmillan Co.,
1916.

Federation of Women Teachers'
Associations of Ontario. *FWTAO
Guidebook.* 1985.

*Friedrich Froebel and English
Education.* Evelyn Lawrence, ed.
London: University of London
Press Ltd., 1952.

Froebel, Friedrich. *Autobiography of
Friedrich Froebel.* Trans. Emile
Michaelis and H. Keatley Moore.
New York: C. W. Berdun Pub.,
1889.

--------. *The Songs and Music of
Friedrich Froebel's Mother Play.*
Prepared and arranged by Susan

E. Blow. New York:
D. Appleton and Co., 1895.

--------. *Pedagogics of the
Kindergarten.* Trans. Josephine
Jarvis. New York: D. Appleton
and Co., 1900.

--------. *Education by Development.*
Trans. Josephine Jarvis.
New York: D. Appleton and Co.,
1902.

--------. *The Education of Man.*
Trans. W. N. Hailmann.
New York: D. Appleton and Co.,
1907.

--------. *Mottoes and Commentaries of
Friedrich Froebel's Mother Play.*
Trans. Henrietta R. Eliot and
Susan E. Blow. New York:
D. Appleton and Co., 1900.

Headley, Neith. *The Kindergarten: Its
Place in the Program of Education.*
New York: The Center for
Applied Research in Education,
Inc., 1965.

Hill, Patty Smith. *Kindergarten.*
Reprint from the *American
Educator Encyclopedia.*
Washington: Association for
Childhood Education, 1942.

Hubbard, Clara Beeson. *Merry Songs
and Games.* New York: Leo
Feist, 1881.

Hughes, James L. *Froebel's
Educational Laws.* New York:
D. Appleton and Co., 1899.

--------. *Dickens as an Educator.*
New York: D. Appleton and Co.,
1913.

--------. James L. *Training the
Children.* New York:
A. S. Barnes Co., 1917.

Kraus-Boelte, Maria; and Kraus,
John. *The Kindergarten Guide.* 2
vols. New York: E. Steiger and
Co., 1882, 1889.

Mann, Mrs. Horace; and Peabody,
Elizabeth P. *Moral Culture of
Infancy and Kindergarten Guide,*
6th ed. New York: J. W.
Schomerhorn and Co., 1876.

Miller, John. *The Educational System
of the Province of Ontario.*
Toronto: Berwick & Sons, 1893.

Montessori, Maria. *The Montessori
Method.* Translated by Anna E.
George. New York: Frederick A.
Stokes Co., 1912.

Pechstein, L. A.; and Jenkins,
Frances. *Psychology of the
Kindergarten-Primary Child.*
Boston: Houghton Mifflin Co.,
1927.

Phillips, Charles E. *The Development
of Education in Canada.* Toronto:
W. J. Gage and Co. Ltd., 1957.

Pierce, Lorne. *Fifty Years of Public
Service.* Toronto: Oxford
University Press, 1924.

*Pioneers of the Kindergarten in
America.* Prepared by the
Committee of Nineteen.

New York: The Century Co.,
1924.

Rusk, Robert R. *A History of Infant
Education.* 2nd ed. London:
University of London Press Ltd.,
1951.

Staff of the Institute of Child Study.
*Twenty-five Years of Child Study
at the Institute of Child Study,
University of Toronto, 1928-
1951.* Edited and chaired by Mary
L. Northway. Toronto: University
of Toronto Press, 1951.

*Webster's Third New International
Dictionary.* Editor-in-Chief Philip
Babcock Gore. Springfield,
Mass.: G. & C. Merriam Co.,
1966.

Articles and Periodicals

Eardley, Kathleen E. "The Free Play
Period in the Kindergarten",*The
School*, XXVII 1938-1939.

Federation of Women Teachers'
Associations of Ontario
(F.W.T.A.O.).Early Childhood
Committee. *Play, Active Learning
in the Early School Years.*
F.W.T.A.O.,1986.

Howarth, M. "How Many Are Too
Many? An Interivew with Otto
Weininger", *F.W.T.A.O.
Newsletter* (February/March
1987).

Maren, Ada. [*sic*] "The Kindergarten
As Related to the Nursery and

School", *Canada School Journal,*
II. (March 1878: 51-53).

Murray, Evelyn. "The Child in the
Kindergarten", *The School,*
XXXV, November 1946.

"Retrospect", *Canada School Journal,*
II (June 1978: 150).

Taylor, E. "Two Hours in a
Kindergarten", *Journal of
Education for Ontario*, XXV
(September 1872).

"The Kindergarten in Canada",
Journal of Education for Ontario,
XXVIII (March 1875: 39-40).

Reports

*An Outline of a Longitudinal Study
from Junior Kindergarten Through
the Elementary Grades.* Research
Report No. 23. Toronto: Board of
Education, 1964.

"Survey of Pre-School Education in
Canada", Research and
Information Division, Canadian
Education Association,
Information Bulletin, No. 1,
Toronto, 1965.

The Kindergarten. Reports of the
Committee of Nineteen of the
International Kindergarten Union
on the Theory and Practice of the
Kindergarten. Boston: Houghton
Mifflin Co., 1913.

Unpublished Material

Johnson, F. H. "Changing Conceptions of Discipline and Pupil-Teacher Relations in Canadian Schools". Unpublished doctoral dissertation, University of Toronto, 1952.

McLaughlin, Paul V. "The Froebelian Movement in the United States". Unpublished doctoral dissertation, University of Ottawa, 1952.

"Maria Kraus-Boelte, in Celebration of Fifty Years of Kindergarten Work – An Account of the Reception Held in New York, December 2, 1969, at the Hotel San Remo".

Mississauga. "Kindergarten Programme". (Mimeographed.)

Ottawa. "Kindergarten Guide Book". (Mimeographed.)

Other Source

Lunde, Laura Hughes, Chicago, Illinois; Correspondence with the author, December 1961 to July 1965.